Summer in the Park

A Musical

Ellen Dryden

A Samuel French Acting Edition

SAMUELFRENCH-LONDON.CO.UK
SAMUELFRENCH.COM

Copyright © 1991 by Ellen Dryden (book) and Don Taylor (lyrics)
All Rights Reserved

SUMMER IN THE PARK is fully protected under the copyright laws of the British Commonwealth, including Canada, the United States of America, and all other countries of the Copyright Union. All rights, including professional and amateur stage productions, recitation, lecturing, public reading, motion picture, radio broadcasting, television and the rights of translation into foreign languages are strictly reserved.

ISBN 978-0-573-08089-0

www.samuelfrench-london.co.uk

www.samuelfrench.com

FOR AMATEUR PRODUCTION ENQUIRIES

UNITED KINGDOM AND WORLD EXCLUDING NORTH AMERICA

plays@SamuelFrench-London.co.uk

020 7255 4302/01

Each title is subject to availability from Samuel French,

depending upon country of performance.

CAUTION: Professional and amateur producers are hereby warned that *SUMMER IN THE PARK* is subject to a licensing fee. Publication of this play does not imply availability for performance. Both amateurs and professionals considering a production are strongly advised to apply to the appropriate agent before starting rehearsals, advertising, or booking a theatre. A licensing fee must be paid whether the title is presented for charity or gain and whether or not admission is charged.

The professional rights in this play are controlled by Casarotto Ramsay Associates, Waverley House, 7-12 Noel Street, London, W1F 8GQ.

No one shall make any changes in this title for the purpose of production. No part of this book may be reproduced, stored in a retrieval system, or transmitted in any form, by any means, now known or yet to be invented, including mechanical, electronic, photocopying, recording, videotaping, or otherwise, without the prior written permission of the publisher. No one shall upload this title, or part of this title, to any social media websites.

The right of Ellen Dryden to be identified as author of this work has been asserted by her in accordance with Section 77 of the Copyright, Designs and Patents Act 1988

SUMMER IN THE PARK

First performed on March 7th to 10th 1990 by Chiswick Youth Theatre, for whose members it was written, at Chiswick Community School, London, and subsequently at the Waterman's Arts Centre, Brentford, from July 17th to 22nd 1990, with the following cast

The Foreground Theatre Company

Katie	Ruth Traynor
Charlotte	Erica Rossi
Nick	Jonathan Taylor
Sophie	Nicola Whitehead
Danny	Jamie Woolgar
Laura	Jackie Chan
Emma	Rachel Warriner
Louise	Hannah Conduct
Amy	Tara Maloney
Sue	Angela Hinds/Lucy Flinders
Tom	Lewis Albrow/Chris Thackray
William & Chris	Andrew Styles
Jack	Max Harvey/Toby Gregory
Michael	Sam Morgan
David	Sam Cocking
Mark	Ben Spencer
Abby	Hannah Murray/Daisy Guard
Joanna	Anna Green
Alice	Jenny Jermain
Zara	Rachel Hillman

The Public

Hilary Osbourne	Juliet Ames-Lewis
Mrs Weekly	Jacky Smith
Mrs Pagett	Tassy Miller
Mr Whittaker	Jeremy St John Smythe/Lincoln Saunders
Zoë Dean	Tami French
Liz Mackie	Anna Durrans
Gary	David Shattu/Darren Carr
Mr Freshwater	Adam Shapiro

The Past

Flora	Natasha Daniels
Abigail	Daisy Guard/Hannah Murray

Musicians Colin Attree, Suzanne Reeves, Helen Sedgwick, Michael Quartey, Sophie Latham, Christina Websdale, Jamie Coleman, Tamsin Alker, Ian Monk, Jonathan West, Lucy Hammond and John Kirby

Technicians Dan Farncombe, Sarah MacCormick, Lucy Taylor, Sarah Kenyon, Naomi Hillman, Joshua Pearcey, Pippa Stockting, Sarah Smith, Natasha Costa Correa, Michael Latham, Sam McCourt, Georgia Hay, Georgina Seal, Nicholas Seal, Ted Sherman, William Sherman, Liza Christie, Ursula Phillips and Andrew Forrer

Designer	Graham Lough
Costume Designer	Rita Reekie
Choreographers	Sheila Falconer, Andrew T. James
Musical Directors	Charles Young, Colin Attree
Directors	Don Taylor, Ellen Dryden, Richard Georgeson

Note on cast. "The Foreground Theatre Company" can be extended by as many extra non-speaking characters – such as Alice and Zara above – as desired.

SUMMER IN THE PARK

ACT I

1. OVERTURE (Music I)
2. SUMMER IN THE PARK (Music II) — Katie
3. IN THE PARK
4. A PATCH OF GREEN (Music III) — Nick, Charlotte and Katie
5. PERSUASION
6. CAN'T BE DONE (Music IV) — Hilary and Company
7. THE WAY THINGS WERE
8. WISTFUL WALTZ (Music V) — Mrs Pagett, Mrs Weekly and Company
9. ENTER MR WHITTAKER
10. BUILDERS (Music VI) — Mr Whittaker and Zoë
11. CLEAN UP THE PARK (Music VII) — Mrs Pagett, Mrs Weekly and Company
12. GOING AWAY
13. LEAVING (Music VIII) — Sophie and Nick
14. BY THE FOUNTAIN
15. FANCY DRESS
16. WHEN YOU'VE GOT THE FROCK (Music IX) — Mark, Amy, Laura and Company
17. STORYTIME
18. LEAVING – *reprise* (Music X) — Sophie
19. MR FRESHWATER
20. FINALE. GET THE PICTURE (Music XI) — Gary, Liz, Zoë, Mr Whittaker, George, Hilary, Mrs Pagett, Mrs Weekly, Chorus

ACT II

21. MINUET (Music XII)
22. FLORA'S TEMPLE
23. WHERE FLORA WALKS (Music XIII) — Nick
24. TECHNICAL
25. IT'LL PROBABLY END IN TEARS (Music XIV) — Amy, Emma, Louise, Laura and Michael
26. FLORA AND ABIGAIL
27. FLORA'S FAREWELL (Music XV) — Flora, Abigail, Nick, Sophie and Katie
28. THE CARD GAME
29. DRINKING SONG (MUSIC XVI) — Danny, Mark, David and Michael

30. HILARY RETURNS
31. FAILURES (Music XVII)   Hilary, Charlotte and Chorus
32. FLORA'S TRAGEDY
33. ELEGY (Music XVIII)   Sophie, Danny, Jack and Flora
34. THE SPIRIT OF THE PLACE
35. SECOND REPRISE OF LEAVING   Flora and Katie
    (Music XIX)
36. GEORGE'S GIFT
37. FLORA'S WALK (Music XX)   Nick
38. AFTER THE STORM
39. THE REAL FLORA (Music XXI)   Flora, Sophie, Katie and Nick
40. THE BATTLE WON ?
41. Finale: SUMMER IN THE PARK   Company
    (Music XXII)

Setting Note
The set as described on page 1 of the text is as it was for the original production. The essentials, however, are a temple, some steps, a fountain, two stone benches and assorted urns. The set can be as formal and elaborately eighteenth century or as simple as resources allow.

Music
The piano/vocal score and associated band parts for this musical are available from Samuel French Ltd.

Production Note
Page 65 (No 35: Second reprise of "Leaving").

If a good "echo" is available in the sound system Flora should not enter at all, and it should be as though Katie were hearing Flora's music all around her in the air. It's even more effective if the sound system has good stereo in the auditorium! Without these technical facilities it is better that Flora should come on stage as indicated.

ACT I

1: Overture (Music I)

A small secluded area in a park; rather wild and overgrown. Daytime

The stage floor is green, representing untended grass. US is a raised section, running the width of the stage. Some stone steps, L, heavily encrusted with moss and debris, run down from it, into a rectangular hollow DS, with a low stone-slabbed wall round it, which contains a little empty ornamental pool, now full of rubbish. At the top of the steps is a broken statue lying on its side, which was obviously once part of a fountain and cascade. Part of the platform US is taken up with a pillared curved structure – a graceful little eighteenth century 'temple'. Balancing the steps R is a low stone balustrade with broken urns which once held flowers

The platform, the temple and the grassy area enclosed by the steps and the balustrade form a natural 'stage', with the temple as the focal point

DS, R and L, are two decorative shrines or niches which once held statues, with little curved stone benches in front of them

There is a suggestion of the skeletal branches of trees and the flat spread of cedars at the side of the stage.

The whole area is an appalling mess. There are drinks cans, crisp packets, plastic bottles, all kinds of household and other rubbish all over the grass, in the pool and in the temple. Every available area of white stone is covered with graffiti. DS, there is a damp mouldering mattress.

The whole place has a run-down, dank, depressed air about it.

   Katie enters slowly, looking round her. The light is pale, glittering and mysterious

2: Summer in the Park (Music II)

Katie   I don't remember it like this,
              Plastic cups and litter,
              Lager cans and paper,
              A forgotten wilderness:
              What happens after dark?
              I remember the magic of summer in the park.

It always seemed a haunted place,
Sighing trees, the glitter
Of a distant, shining river:
Sunlight, silence, space,
White temples in the dark.
A childhood dream of summer in the park.

Nothing whispers in the trees:
The spirits are leaving,
The temples decaying:
Time passes like a breeze,
Till there's nothing left but the dark.
Why can't it always be summer in the park?

3: In the Park

Nick and Charlotte enter

The Lights cross-fade to a blue sky effect

Charlotte looks round, eagerly at first, then with increasing disgust

Katie watches Nick anxiously

Charlotte The answer is No. No. And No, in that order.
Nick (*levelly*) I see.
Katie (*looking round*) Oh, Charlotte, why? (*During the following, she takes very little notice of Charlotte and Nick*)
Charlotte No, I don't want to co-produce a play with Nick – because we couldn't even agree on the colour of the tickets! No, I don't want to get involved in anything organized by Hilary Osbourne. No, I don't think this would make a very glamorous setting for a play. (*She looks round*) And No. And No. (*She picks up one corner of the mattress with extreme distaste. She shudders and lets it fall, then wipes her fingers fastidiously*) I think the council tip would make a better setting. In fact are you sure this isn't the tip? Only someone with the brains of a mentally defective woodlouse would even consider it. And there's plenty of those under that mattress so why don't you join them?
Nick Have you finished?
Charlotte I could go on. But is it worth it? When you were all banging on about Freshwater Park, I thought it would be something. This isn't much bigger than our back garden.
Nick We're not all as privileged as you though, Charlotte. Seems quite big to us peasants.
Katie I haven't been here since I was little. I thought it was enormous then. . . It used to be a short cut to my primary school. It was always kept quite nice though. We used to come here on sunny afternoons – and count the snails! (*With a grin*) I've drawn pictures of Class Seven in here on a nature trail! (*She wanders down to the fountain*)

Act I

Charlotte (*acidly*) Let's all stroll down Memory Lane! I'm happy to say that this is my first and last visit. It's a hopeless dump. A forgotten little corner that time has passed by and so will we!

Nick That's the point. This is all that's left. This bit is exactly one ninth of the original park. The estate covered the whole area. The house was bang in the middle – where the roundabout is now. And there were nine of these walks going out from the house – like a sort of nine-pointed star. And there were temples to the Nine Muses at the end of each alley of trees.

Charlotte Why?

Nick The eighteenth century was like that. The whole place was dedicated to Art and Music. Wonder what this temple was for?

Charlotte A public lavatory judging by the smell! It's dedicated to glue-sniffers and winoes now, isn't it? Come on let's go before we catch something!

Nick You can't just let them barge in and knock it all down though, can you?

Katie I like it here. It's got atmosphere.

Charlotte That's not atmosphere. That's plain old-fashioned stink!

Nick It's the last bit of character left round here. If this goes it'll just be row upon row of tacky houses —

Katie Nobody would be able to use it —

Charlotte Nobody uses it now.

Katie I think it's sad that this is all that's left, and people can't be bothered.

Charlotte The gospel according to Hilary Osbourne! You're not going to be crazy enough to get involved in one of her crackbrained schemes, are you? You know what she'll do? She'll get you in so deep you can't get out and she'll be off knitting blankets for the whales in the rain forests, and leave you to clear up the mess.

Katie (*not sounding convinced*) That's not fair. She's really nice. She does a lot of good. And she gets things going —

Charlotte For five minutes. She's got a letter in the local paper about a different issue each week. She gets all worked up, gets everybody else roped in, then *she* moves on to something else.

Nick You could say it's her job to get things stirred up.

Katie Yes, I agree with Nick. She couldn't do everything herself.

Charlotte Little Miss Echo! Nick's little shadow! You are allowed to have an idea that Nick hasn't already had first you know, Katie.

Nick Shut up, Charlotte, don't be childish.

Katie (*wincing*) I'm sorry, Nick.

Nick (*irritated*) Don't *you* apologize, for God's sake.

There is a slight pause

Charlotte Look, we've just managed to get a decent bit of money together. We don't want to chuck it all away. If we're landed with doing a play here, and then Hilary's off onto her next burning issue, and leaves us in the lurch, we could lose a lot of money.

Nick Or make a lot. You could get a much bigger audience here —
Charlotte Are you going to offer them typhoid jabs with their programmes?
Nick Look, the others will be here in a minute. Let's just get their reactions straight shall we?
Charlotte I have not said a word to anybody – yet. And you're already getting at me!
Nick Oh come on! If they think you're against it half of them will just pull out all together.
Charlotte And what about the other half? *You* don't influence anybody of course!
Katie I think it's good here . . . it's sort of romantic.
Charlotte Romantic! You're mad!
Katie No – it could be quite mysterious. . . It'd be lovely for night scenes, with a harvest moon. . .
Charlotte In June?
Katie We'd need to do a bit of clearing up.
Charlotte You can say that again!
Nick It's been locked up for ages.
Charlotte Yes, to keep the derelicts out!
Nick No, it's like everything else. If you're not sure what to do with something lock it away.
Charlotte Well, if I'm absolutely honest with you, I think it's probably the best thing to do with it – bulldoze it and build some decent houses – with nice gardens! I mean the site must be worth a fortune. It could be really attractive. The rest of the park's gone. Why make a fuss about this little bit? It's shut away, closed up and filthy dirty. Muddy bit of river down one end and the main road the other, houses all round. Most people don't even know it's here.
Nick That's because nobody's told them it's theirs!

4: A Patch of Green (Music III)

(*Singing*)   Why squander a patch of green,
A dome of sky, an arc of sun,
Why destroy what the past has given
To everyone.
Why abolish a green space,
A temple dome, a river walk?
Must we concrete over the whole place?
This is our park.

Simultaneously Charlotte and Katie sing

Charlotte		Katie	
	Don't waste your time,		The temples decaying,
	Beyond repair,		The river walk
	Forgotten dream,		The dreams are going,
	Castles in the air.		Summer in the park.

Act I

Charlotte   It won't work, don't waste your time,
            The place a ruin, beyond repair,
            A dead dreamer's forgotten dream,
            Castles in the air.
            Look at it now, a wasteland,
            Overgrown grass, a crumbled heap
            Of plaster and stucco, and a bandstand
            Where the derelicts sleep.

Simultaneously Nick and Katie sing

Katie	The temples decaying,	Nick	A patch of green,
	The river walk,		An arc of sun
	The dreams are going,		The past has given
	Summer in the park.		To everyone.

Katie   The spirits are leaving, the temples decaying,
        The white domes, the river walk;
        The dream is dying, the dreamers are going;
        Summer in the park.
        People have walked here, lived and loved here,
        In Spring morning and Autumn dark;
        Where are they now, what have they left here?
        Summer in the park.

Simultaneously Nick and Charlotte sing

Nick	A patch of green,	Charlotte	Don't waste your time,
	An arc of sun		Beyond repair,
	The past has given		Forgotten dream,
	To everyone.		Castles in the air.
	Summer in the park		

5: Persuasion

Mrs Hilary Osbourne enters as the song comes to an end

A group of young people: Sophie, Laura, Louise, Emma, Amy, Joanna, Abby, Sue, William, Michael, Tom, David, Jack, Mark, Chris and Danny follow her. They look around with some interest, as they are obviously here for the first time

Hilary Oh good, you got here. I wondered if you'd be able to get away. The gates were already open were they?
Nick Yeah.
Hilary Well that's something, I suppose. Those gates have been padlocked for four years to my certain knowledge. We've been pestering the Town Hall – somebody must have actually listened to us.
Charlotte How do you know they've opened them for us? They were wide open – might have been for the bulldozers.
Nick That's right, look on the bright side.

Hilary No, they can't do anything before the inquiry. But you're quite right, I expect the developers will be in here working – sizing things up. It's very important for us to get going. (*Energetically*) Now, I've been putting these chaps in the picture. There wasn't much more to say in your stuffy old rehearsal room. So here we are. Nicholas. Have you persuaded Charlotte yet? I think *we're* all of one mind. . .
Charlotte What a surprise! What makes you think I need to be persuaded?
Hilary Oh, come on, Charlotte. You're our resident pessimist! That's why you're invaluable! You can ferret out all the snags.
Charlotte And you can steamroller them!
Hilary That's it. Teamwork.
Charlotte Why don't you just stand in front of the bulldozers when they come?
Hilary It might come to that!
Charlotte Bad luck the bulldozers.
Hilary Are we agreed then? Nick? Sophie?
Charlotte Hang on!
Katie (*decisively*) I think. . . Well, I think we should – (*Losing her nerve*) what do you think Nick?
Nick (*slowly*) Well – we haven't decided what we're doing next. We were going to do a modern play but —
Charlotte You couldn't do that here.
Danny It would depend on the play —
Sophie Name me three modern plays that require an overgrown park with vandalized eighteenth century temples as the setting.
Danny I don't know anything about plays. I just do what I'm told.
Laura Anyway, we always do our shows in St. Thomas's Hall.
Hilary Don't you think it could be very exciting? It could be the centre piece of the whole campaign. Think about it – special gala performances in the park. We could end with fireworks, music – wine – a party even. We'd fill the place. And it would really give the campaign a focus. Much better than endless petitions.
Emma What if it rains?
Hilary Well, yes – but it wouldn't rain every night. And if it did we could move into the Church Hall.
Danny Can I do the fireworks in the Church Hall?
Louise What do you want us to do? Shakespeare?.
Emma You could do *Midsummer Night's Dream*, I suppose. . .
Laura They always do that in Courtlees Park.
Hilary No, I'll tell you what we'll do.
Charlotte I thought you might.
Hilary This place is brimming with history – fascinating stories – I haven't gone into it yet – but you could do that. The clever thing would be to do your own play.

They all look at Hilary

You'd like to produce that wouldn't you, Charlotte?
Charlotte I'm not co-directing with Nick – it wouldn't work.

Act I

Hilary No, Nick would write it.
Nick Gee, thanks!
Hilary Sophie would research it. Oh and er – Katie. Amy would design it.
Amy Nice to be asked.
Hilary Chris light it —
Tom I'll do the sound.
Hilary – and so on. That would get the campaign off to a terrific start. Show them we mean business.
Sue Where do we rehearse?
Hilary Oh here. As much as we can.
Sue That means we have to drag all the props here every rehearsal.
Chris And the lights. Can't do a lighting rig in five minutes.
Sue How do we get all the stuff here?
Michael I can guess.
David Mike's van!! And he can give us all a lift —
Mark And run us all down to the Pub if it rains!
Danny Then come back for the gear!
Sophie And what would you do?
Hilary Make an almighty nuisance of myself – to the developers, I mean!
Nick (*With a grin*) No? Really?
Hilary Think of me as a battering ram —
Charlotte If you insist!
Hilary –I'll smash our way in. You take over.

6: Can't be Done (Music IV)

(*Singing*)   For an action group or a standing committee
You won't find anyone better than me.
To stop a road or save an inner city
Needs my kind of energy.
We could make your play a great occasion,
And give the builders one in the eye.
Plays are the jolliest form of persuasion.
Why not give it a try?

As each solo line is sung, it is immediately echoed by the chorus

Emma	Can't be done.
Jack	Isn't worth it.
Louise	Not a chance.
Michael	Won't work.
Amy	Not much fun.
Tom	Let's forget it.
Laura	Take a glance.
David	Scrub the park!
Chris	Too much hassle.
Sue	Drive us crazy.
Mark	No one asked her.
Abby	Cause a row.

William	Mega trouble.
Joanna	All go barmy.
Danny	Hallo disaster.
All	Junk it now, junk it now!

The music continues as Hilary speaks

Hilary You were going to do a play anyway. Just do it here. Do your play for a purpose, not just for yourselves. (*She begins singing the second verse*)

> It can be done, of course it's worth doing,
> There's every chance we can make it work.
> We'll make it such fun you'll never forget it,
> One glance will save the park!
> Life is all hassle, the way to go crazy
> Is to ask for nothing, dodge every row.
> If you don't look for trouble, you *will* go barmy.
> Disaster to stop us now.

As each solo line is sung, it is immediately echoed by the chorus

Emma	Why not?
Jack	She's good news.
Louise	Take a chance.
Michael	Quite a girl!
Amy	Do the lot.
Tom	Nothing to lose.
Laura	Make 'em dance.
David	Give it a whirl!
Chris	Stuff the council!
Sue	Stuff the critics!
Mark	Stuff the builders!
Abby	Show them how!
William	Guts an' bounce'll
Joanna	Beat statistics.
Danny	Art enraptures.
All	Let's start now, let's start now!
(*singing together*)	Let's go for it then, we'll do it together
	You make the speeches and we'll do the play.
	Put up the posters and pray for good weather
	And hope it all comes right on the day.
	Long live the drama, long live the players,
	Speak to the people as plays always should.
	Down with developers, creeps and betrayers,
	Stand by Beginners, it had better be good!
	Why not?
	She's good news.
	Take a chance.
	Quite a girl!

Act I

>Do the lot.
>Nothing to lose.
>Make 'em dance.
>Give it a whirl!
>Stuff the council!
>Stuff the critics!
>Stuff the builders!
>Show them how!
>Guts an' bounce'll
>Beat statistics.
>Art enraptures.
>Let's start now, let's start now!

7: The Way Things Were

At the end of the song the group disperses round the stage investigating the area

The younger boys, Jack, William and Tom, are specially interested in the steps and the broken fountain

>*Mrs Weekly and Mrs Pagett, two old ladies, enter with their shopping. They stare with unconcealed curiosity at Hilary and the group of young people.*

Mrs Weekly There you are you see! I told you they'd come down and opened them gates. When I went out for Ron's paper I saw the man. Very offhand he was.

Mrs Pagett Did you speak to him?

Mrs Weekly Yes, I said "What are you doing?", and he said "I'm unlocking the gates. What do you think I'm doing, flying to the moon?". I says "Why?". He says "Because I bin told". I says "Can we go in then?". He says "I dunno. I've just bin told to open the gates. Dunno what for."! I says "Didn't you ask why?". He says "No, I couldn't care less." Then he says "T'ra Gran" and gets on his bike and rides off. One of those horrible little pop-pop motor bikes it was. *And* he rode halfway down to the corner on the pavement. Spotty Herbert he was an' all. Didn't look no more than twenty. And that's what they call a council official!

Mrs Pagett Oh I know, you don't have to tell me. That's the trouble these days. When I got on to them – about the teenagers round our way they couldn't have cared less.

Mrs Weekly It's the same up the cemetery. Terrible!

Hilary Hallo.

Mrs Weekly Morning. Are you from the council?

Hilary Oh no.

Mrs Weekly All this lot – are they with you? Are you doing nature study – a survey or something?

Hilary Er no, not exactly.

Mrs Weekly That's all people do nowadays. When they see a mess they do a survey instead of setting to and clearing it up. Go round counting the flowers in the park! Don't pull up any weeds or pick up the litter! Just put up fiddly little trees for people to knock down.

Mrs Pagett Yes, do you know, they've planted a cherry tree down our turning *four* times. Built a great fence round it and it still gets smashed up. I don't know what people are coming to. Kids it is. Little kid the other day – only about eight he was – went down our road just knocking the heads off of all the flowers with this gun thing. Wanton destruction that's what it was.

Mrs Weekly and Mrs Pagett shake their heads at the wickedness of the world

There is a momentary sadness

Hilary (*briskly*) Oh no! We are going to stop the destruction. We – that is, *I* — am on the committee to save this park from the developers. Did you know they were going to build houses on it?

Mrs Weekly Oh yes, it was in the local paper... They won't be houses for *people* though will they?

Mrs Pagett Yes, ridiculous price they're going to be. Ordinary people can't pay those prices.

Mrs Weekly Typical. Now if they was to build houses —

Hilary We don't think they should build anything. We think they should leave the park as it is.

Mrs Weekly As it is!!

Mrs Pagett Leave it like this??

Hilary Well, cleared up obviously – that's were we come in.

Hilary gestures round but the group of young people is scattered around the park taking little or no notice of her and the two old ladies

Mrs Weekly Now this place really used to be something when I was a girl. I lived just over there and we used to come here of an evening.

Mrs Pagett It was really lovely.

Mrs Weekly Grass like a billiard table. Not a blade out of place. And of a Sunday there used to be a band over there – used to play waltzes. Strauss waltzes... (*She gestures towards the temple*)

Mrs Pagett Or sometimes it was the Salvation Army. Used to play hymns —

Mrs Weekly People used to come in and sit on the grass or walk down by the river.

Mrs Pagett There used to be a little tea stall. Small, but very clean. Over by the gates.

Mrs Weekly And there was none of them paper cups either. People had a decent cup of tea in a proper cup and saucer. *And* they took them back to the stall when they'd finished!

Mrs Pagett Everybody dressed up properly as well. The boys would wear their good suits. And we used to do ourselves up smashing. I had a lovely cream shantung frock. Oh, I didn't half fancy myself in that, I can tell you!

Mrs Weekly And you didn't get any of these kids with their knees poking out of them horrible jeans!

Mrs Pagett In those days you didn't get people with enough money to know

Act I   11

better going round with their bums out of their trousers! And you had people that were *really* poor then. But they kept themselves respectable.
Mrs Weekly We didn't go round writing on walls either.
Mrs Pagett No, we had a bit of respect – not like now.
Mrs Weekly We knew how to enjoy ourselves, we did.

8: Wistful Waltz (Music V)

Mrs Pagett (*singing*)	When I was a girl, this place was a picture.
Mrs Weekly	When I was a girl it was really nice.
Mrs Pagett	You could stroll of a Sunday, and it was a pleasure.
Mrs Weekly	You didn't need asking to come here twice.
Mrs Pagett	The music was lovely.
Mrs Weekly	The Salvation Army.
Mrs Pagett	Sometimes we had singers.
Mrs Weekly	We danced on the grass.
Mrs Pagett	You came as a family.
Mrs Weekly	Dad's hair greased and smarmy.
Mrs Pagett	With the pram and the baby.
Mrs Weekly	The place had some class.
Mrs Pagett	The beauty.
Mrs Weekly	The laughter.
Mrs Pagett	The past.
Mrs Weekly	We were young.
Mrs Pagett	Like poetry.
Mrs Weekly	Like water.
Mrs Pagett	Goes so fast.
Mrs Weekly	Gone so long.
Mrs Pagett	We lived for the weekend.
Mrs Weekly	Tomorrow was never.
Mrs Pagett	Our legs in silk stockings.
Mrs Weekly	Our hair set in curls.
Mrs Pagett }	We wanted the party to go on for ever.
Mrs Weekly }	Life danced in waltz time when we were both girls.
Mrs Weekly	But now it's all beer cans, and jeans and graffiti.
Mrs Pagett	And portable radios that make you go deaf.
Mrs Weekly	They smoke, they take drugs, and they never have P.T.
Mrs Pagett	They swear at their teachers and beat up the ref.
Mrs Weekly	They never do homework.
Mrs Pagett	Or help their poor mothers.
Mrs Weekly	They're dirty and lazy.
Mrs Pagett	And dressed in old rags,
Mrs Weekly	After dark they go berserk
Mrs Pagett	And mug their grandmothers,
Mrs Weekly	And drive themselves crazy
Mrs Pagett	With lager and fags.

Mrs Weekly	They're vandals
Mrs Pagett	Disgusting.
Mrs Weekly	They're thick.
Mrs Pagett	Got no brains.
Mrs Weekly	Like animals.
Mrs Pagett	Degrading
Mrs Weekly	They're sick,
Mrs Pagett	Minds like drains.

The Chorus sings a counter-melody as Mrs Pagett and Mrs Weekly continue

Chorus   Vandals, Vandals,
No brains in their head.
Even the animals
Don't soil their own bed.
Vandals, Vandals,
Uncivilized, apart:
Burning the citadels
Of everyone's heart

Mrs Weekly	We never had Vandals in our day.
Mrs Pagett	No fear!
Mrs Weekly	We had some respect for things.
Mrs Pagett	Knew right from wrong.
Mrs Weekly ⎫	We had fun, we hurt nobody, year after year.
Mrs Pagett ⎭	The world was much nicer when we were both young.

The chorus repeats the counter-melody, while Mrs Weekly and Mrs Pagett sing their melody to "LA LA LA"

9: Enter Mr Whittaker

Mr Whittaker, a shiny young man in a suit, enters from behind the temple as the song ends. He has a briefcase and a polaroid camera. He smiles briefly at the group, moves and photographs the derelict fountain and the little shrines

Zoë, a young woman, as glamorous as he is shiny, accompanies him

Mr Whittaker Good-morning.

The group mutter "good-morning" suspiciously. They do not like the look of him

    Do excuse me. . . I'm so sorry. . . Could I just ask you to move slightly? I need to take a shot of that pavilion affair and I don't want any people in it. Not this picture at any rate.

The group move aside resentfully

Mrs Pagett Do you want us in the next one then?

Mr Whittaker That would be charming, but I'm afraid I'm just here to photograph the – buildings. . .

Hilary *(quietly)* The *site*!

Act I   13

There is an angry murmur from the group

Mrs Weekly You from the paper?
Mr Whittaker Oh no, no. It's sad to see things in this condition, isn't it?
Hilary Very. You wouldn't be from Gresham Developments by any chance would you?
Mr Whittaker Ah, how very astute of you. Yes and no. And you – what? Local residents taking advantage of the park being opened again after so long?
Hilary Yes – and no!
Nick Have you been here all morning?
Mr Whittaker Yes, I was down by the river. It's very beautiful there. Very peaceful and secluded. There was a ground mist earlier on. The temple looked as if it were floating. I think I saw a heron.
Hilary Do we have you to thank for the gates being opened?
Mr Whittaker Oh no. Not entirely. That was as much for your benefit as mine. It is still a public space. It should never have been locked up in the first place.
Hilary But if Greshams have their way the Keep Out notices and the Guard Dogs will be here any day now.
Mr Whittaker Ah! Am I right in thinking that you are – the opposition to the Gresham plan?
Hilary Yes, you are. Quite right.
Mrs Weekly No you're not. Not about me. I don't know anything about it.
Mrs Pagett I'm not opposed to anything.
Nick How many houses do you reckon they'll build here?
Mr Whittaker Oh, I couldn't possibly say. I'm not part of the architectural or the construction side. And of course, it hasn't been decided yet whether any houses will be built or not. It's only a proposal.
Nick What sort of houses will they be?
Mr Whittaker (*smiling*) Good ones.
Nick (*resenting being patronised*) Who for? They're demolishing the tower blocks on the Abbeyfield Estate. Will they be for the people from there?
Mr Whittaker Er, certainly, if they wish to buy them.
Nick They'll be really cheap then?
Mr Whittaker (*levelly*) They will be architecturally pleasing houses at competitive prices, for people who are prepared to pay for quality.
Nick Thought so.
Hilary Why is it so difficult to find out anything about all this? Why are you being so secretive?
Mr Whittaker Everything is at a very early stage yet. Greshams intend to be absolutely above board in every aspect. This is a very sensitive issue. The full, whole-hearted co-operation of the community is vital to the scheme's success – if it is to happen at all.
Danny What are you taking all the pictures for?
Mr Whittaker Oh, I'm just here on a kind of recce. To get some idea of the area. In answer to your worries – Miss? —
Hilary Osbourne. *Mrs* Osbourne.

Mr Whittaker makes to shake hands with her with careful sincerity

Hilary takes his hand briefly

Mr Whittaker Whittaker. Giles Whittaker — and this is my Personal Assistant —

Zoë (*smiling glacially*) How do you do.

Mr Whittaker We shall be providing a very comprehensive brochure, lavishly illustrated of course. (*With an ingratiating smile at his use of the cliché*) Setting out all the options — photographs, exhibitions, models —

Hilary Taking note of objections?

Mr Whittaker Of course! (*Talking to the group at large*) We must work together in this — Mrs Osbourne, all of you. After all we want the same thing. The best possible use of this lovely space, for the benefit of the local community at large. We shouldn't see ourselves as enemies.

10:Builders (Music VI)

Mr Whittaker
Zoë

Builders, serving
The general good
Creating something
Where nothing stood.
Building tomorrow
Here today.
Pay cash or borrow,
Suits us either way.

Builders, making
Your dreams come true;
Only taking
A percentage or two.
The park's day is over,
It's gone, let it go.
We are the future.
Invest in us now.

The music continues as Mr Whittaker speaks over it

Mr Whittaker What we can offer you is what you want — planned with care, designed with flair at a price that reassures you that what you are buying is unashamed luxury. A home that shows the world just what you are worth.

Mr Whittaker and Zoë reprise verse two, while the company sings a shortened version of the "VANDALS" chorus of Music V

Mr Whittaker
Zoë

Builders, making
Your dreams come true;
Only taking
A percentage or two
The park's day is over,
It's gone, let it go.
We are the future.
Invest in us now.

Act I 15

Company Vandals, vandals.
Vandals, vandals,
Burning the citadels
Of everyone's heart.

Mr Whittaker I'm sure we shall meet again. Meanwhile please don't hesitate to get in touch with me, whenever you want any information. There is no need for us to fight over this scheme. (*Silkily*) I would hate you to be under any misapprehensions.
Hilary Really?
Mr Whittaker (*sincerely*) Now that I've met you, Mrs Osbourne, I don't want to see you – how shall I put it? – attacking us on mistaken assumptions. That would be so embarrassing (*he pauses*). For you. Let's be civilised and – friendly – shall we?

Mr Whittaker gives Hilary his card

Hilary (*wryly*) Thank you. I don't have a card I'm afraid. Not in this capacity—
Mr Whittaker Let us hope you never need one. Good-morning. So nice to have met you all.

Mr Whittaker exits with Zoë, leaving Hilary staring ruefully at his card

Danny What a creep!
Mrs Weekly I think he was a very nice, polite, well-spoken young man.
Mrs Pagett At least he'd got a bit of time for you —

Mrs Weekly and Mrs Pagett sit a little way away from the group

Hilary That's his job. He's a Public Relations man. That's what he's here for. To sell us Gresham's scheme.
Katie Why was he taking all those pictures?
Danny Yeah! With that rubbishy little camera?
Laura They won't be any good in a brochure.
David Probably taking lousy pictures now to show what a dump it it – then they'll come up with a marvellous artist's impression of what it could be like – before and after.
Danny No, he said he was recceing the place. If he's the P.R. man he's not going to be the photographer as well. They'll be in here taking hundreds of arty shots for their brochure. Make it look really dire.
Hilary You're probably right. One of the problems is, the place is so run down. It's difficult to make a case for keeping it untouched!
Nick Who's responsible for it?
Hilary That's a bit of a mystery. Sir Joshua Freshwater built it – the council have administered it for years, through a sort of trust, but it doesn't belong to them. They're just caretakers.
David And a lovely job they've made of it.
Hilary They can't afford to restore it – anyway, it's not their job – they just want to be rid of the responsibility.
Danny How can they build on it if nobody knows who it belongs to?

Hilary Well, the Freshwaters used to own all the land round here – most of it was sold off years ago – so I suppose it belongs to the family. But I don't even know if there are any descendants... We're trying to find out who it belongs to. So are Greshams. That's why we need to make a big effort. If we can trace the owner we need to show him – or her – that we care about the place – that it matters to us all. And that we *use* it. So that's why we need you. If we can start our campaign with a splash – with a show from you – well, we can get hold of the public and get them on our side before Greshams.
Charlotte That's asking a bit much – our pathetic little show against their publicity department. And don't say David and Goliath or I shall throw up.
Hilary I wouldn't dream of it, but you've got the advantage of being local. They're outsiders. And if we can get people annoyed about decisions being taken over their heads *and* about having their park taken away from them —
Charlotte To build houses —

There are cries of derision from the group

Nick Come off it, Charlotte, you saw the oil slick just now. He's not one of the world's benefactors is he?
Joanna But if nobody knows who it belongs to how can it be the people's park?
Hilary It just always has been – till they locked it up.
Laura Well– (*to the others*) what do you think? We're going to do a play anyway. Might as well be here.
Charlotte (*with heavy irony*) Hey kids – let's do the show here!!!
Danny It'd be different. Come on Charlotte.
Charlotte I'm not saying no. Anyway, if Nick's decided that's it, isn't it?
Louise Have we got permission?
Hilary Oh yes, it's a free for all, but we've got exclusive use of the park for four nights in June.
Emma Usually rains all through June.
Danny Then we'll put up a tent.
Abby What are we going to do?
Nick Write our own show.
Charlotte What about?
Nick (*gravely*) Oh, about the decline of community spirit. The problems of the modern teenager *vis-à-vis* his or her social and cultural environment and the difficulties encountered in getting a good rock band on the road.
Charlotte (*drily*) Why did I ask?
Katie I think we should do something romantic – midsummer in the moonlight – I'd like to wear a long floating white dress and come drifting up from the river through the mist.
Danny Why not go drifting *into* the river – and just keep walking?
Tom (*thoughtfully*) What are *they* going to do while we're here? We'd better keep an eye on them, hadn't we?
Jack Yeah, what if they try to spoil everything? What if they try to set something up while *we're* here?
Hilary Don't worry about that, I'll set my committee onto it. And I shall keep

Act I

in *close* touch with – (*consulting the card*) Mr Whittaker!
Tom If he wants loads of pictures to show everybody what a dump this is, why don't we clear it up – so it isn't?

The group look at Tom

David That's not a bad idea.
Hilary It's a very good idea.
Jack Would we be allowed?
Hilary (*crossing her fingers*) Oh yes! Anyway, who's going to object to anyone scrubbing off all this mess and restoring the place to its former glory?
Danny Mr Oily Whittaker?
Tom Can we clean those steps? You ought to be able to get a fountain going again there. That's what they're for.
Hilary Well I don't know about that.

Mrs Weekly and Mrs Pagett rejoin the group

Mrs Weekly That's the best idea anybody's had this morning. You get on with it. I reckon cleaning up all this mess is the best thing you could do.
Mrs Pagett Yes, it could do with a good clean-up.
Mrs Weekly It's you youngsters have made all the mess in the first place. Us old folks don't go round scribbling on everything.

11: Clean Up the Park (Music VII)

Company	Clean up the park,
	Clean up the park,
	Till it looks like new.
	We'll make a schedule and put the temple
	Number one on the list.
	We'll make no treaty with those graffiti,
	They won't ever be missed.
	We'll need a basket, with such a task it
	'S crucial to make a plan.
	Don't miss a thing,
	Paper or string.
Mrs Pagett **Mrs Weekly** (*together*)	Try elbow grease, if your sort can!
Company	We must be thorough, and show the whole borough
	How the job should be done.
	A sack for the paper, a brush and a scraper
	Halves the work and doubles the fun.
	With organisation the transformation
	Will need seeing to be believed.
	From being a tip
	With work and a skip
	The poor old park will be reprieved
	Yes, the poor old park will be reprieved.

                        We'll scrape the fountain, and make a mountain
                        Of green moss on the grass.
                        We'll give it a go till our fingers glow
                        And the steps are smooth as glass.
                        We've got to be drastic, all this old plastic
                        Where the coke cans and chip papers lurk
                        In piles round the back
                        We'll put in a sack.

Mrs Pagett
Mrs Weekly } (*together*) It'll make a change to see you work!

Company   It's time to begin it, if we want to win it
                The battle starts now and here.
                We'll get the place mended and make it look splendid
                As in its foundation year.
                So if the first owner should ever return, a
                Big smile would spread on his face.
                "Good heavens, they've swept it,
                And scrubbed it and kept it
                Just how I remember the dear old place,
                Just how I remember the dear old place."

                Don't wait till it's dark,
                Let's clean up the park,
                Till it looks like new.
                Till-it-looks-like-NEW.

Everyone exits, except Nick and Sophie who are left alone on the stage

12: Going Away

Sophie Aren't you going with them?
Nick No, I'll leave the menial work to the others. My job is to be the creative powerhouse behind this little artistic venture.
Sophie (*with disgust*) Oh God, Nick!
Nick Joke?!
Sophie If you say so. You don't make *me* laugh.
Nick Aren't you going to help them then? You're a real wiz at cleaning everything up. With your spit they wouldn't need paint stripper.
Sophie I don't know whether I'll still be here in June.

There is a pause

Nick You're still set on going then?
Sophie And you're still set on staying!
Nick (*expansively*) I like it here!
Sophie Oh yes, I've noticed! I don't though. I hate it. Why should I bother to help save anything here? What's this place ever done for me? It's all right for you. And Mrs Osbourne. She's got a nice little place down by

Act I

the river, hasn't she? With a lovely garden with old-fashioned roses and peach trees. Nice for her to come for a stroll here in the evening, isn't it? And feel good because, single-handed, she's saved this beautiful park from the wicked developers. It doesn't look the same if you live in a stinking little sixth floor flat overlooking the railway. Wormwood Scrubs without the charm! Mum and me wouldn't mind a nice little place here I can tell you!

Nick You and Mummy wouldn't be able to afford Gresham's prices.

Sophie That's all you know! My mum can afford anything now she's going to marry 'Uncle' Trevor! He's going to give her the sun and the moon and the stars – and that's just for breakfast! (*She starts to leave*)

Nick Don't go.

Sophie Why not?

Nick Just don't. Don't rush off in a mood. It's a nice day.

She returns giving him a sceptical look

They remain silent for a moment

Sophie Well, this is fun isn't it?

Nick I shall miss you – if you go for good.

Sophie Why?

Nick I like talking to you.

They both explode with laughter

Nick Why Newcastle?

Sophie Because they've offered me a place – and because it's three hundred miles away from Mum and Uncle Trevor and because – perhaps – people up there don't go around being hypocritical all the time and pretending we're all nice middle-class people with nice middle-class manners!

Nick No, they go around pretending they're all professional Geordies!

Sophie It'd make a change.

Nick What do you want a change for? You've got a fantastic job – which you like. Why do you want to play at being a student?

Sophie Because I'm pig ignorant, aren't I? But I'm not stupid. I couldn't wait to get out of school when I was sixteen. Perhaps that was the first of my mistakes... I haven't made my mind up yet, anyway. I might go anywhere. I just want – out!

Nick You don't think there's anything to keep you here?

Sophie looks at him and shrugs

Sophie *You* ought to get away.

Nick Why? For the good of my soul? I'm comfortable here.

Sophie That the trouble. You're so lazy! You're really quite bright – and you don't do anything. I wish I'd got half your brains.

Nick shrugs and moves away

Nick (*bitterly*) You don't need them with your – energy!
Sophie You shouldn't stay here Nick. You shouldn't settle for being a big fish in a tiny pond.
Nick Clang!
Sophie What?
Nick Thundering cliché. No, you see the Bad Fairy came to my christening and said "He will be bright but he won't be bothered!" So I pricked my finger and fell asleep for the next hundred years.
Sophie And you're waiting for the Princess to hack her way through the thorn-bushes and wake you with a kiss?!
Nick Or the Prince!

Sophie looks at him sadly

(*Striking a pose*) Oh God! What am I doing with my life?
Sophie Many a true word spoken in jest. Cliché!
Nick I shall miss you. Help us with our little play – before you go —
Sophie It's a waste of time and energy really though isn't it? We're not going to make a scrap of difference.
Nick Now you're talking like Charlotte.
Sophie No I'm not. She only does it to be difficult. I mean it.
Nick I wish you'd stay though.
Sophie I've got nothing to stay for. And there's too much to get away from.

13: Leaving (Music VIII)

(*singing*) My mother and her fella
I suppose they think I'm blind,
And I haven't the guts to tell her
Just what I'm leaving behind.
Nothing in that dreary flat,
Nothing in the street.
Something like nothing in my heart:
Something that feels like defeat.

So soon I'll be leaving
For some better place.
Seeing is believing
And that same old face
Looks at me every morning
In the mirror, so leave her there.
Just go, without any warning,
Somewhere, anywhere.

Nick That face in the mirror,
You can't leave it behind.
The next bathroom you enter
It's her reflection you'll find.
Nothing isn't a fact of place,

Act I   21

>   Nothing's a state of mind.
>   You won't change the look of your face
>   By pretending to be blind.
>
>   And what are you missing
>   By never staying long?
>   Something slowly passing,
>   Like a snatch of some old half-forgotten song,
>   A tune you can't quite remember,
>   A poem that said it all.
>   That chance will be gone forever
>   When you slam the door in the hall.

Sophie   I must believe that living
                 Is meant to be more than this.
                 Doing and loving and giving
                 And I'm not prepared to miss
                 Any possible chance of finding
                 The life that I know must be there
                 So I have to leave, and I'm going,
                 Somewhere, anywhere.

Sophie repeats her last verse while Nick sings the following in counterpoint

Nick   Something passes
                 When people go,
                 When people go,
                 Something more is leaving,
                 Oh, something more is leaving
                 Than either of us –
                 Either of us – can know.

Nick and Sophie sing in Duet

Sophie	Leaving,	**Nick**	Leaving,
	Going away.		Drifting apart.
	Leaving,		Leaving,
	Nothing to stay for.		What if your heart says
	Parting,		Stay here,
	Waving goodbye,		Give it a chance,
	Going,		Don't go,
	Heaven knows why, but		Even a trance-like
	Leaving,		Dreaming
	Going away,		's an honester way
	Leaving,		Than going
	Soon.		Too soon.

Sophie and Nick exit in opposite directions

14: By The Fountain

The Lights change to a misty grey dawn with the pink gold hint of a beautiful day

The dawn chorus is almost over

    Tom, Jack and William enter quietly and cautiously. They are carrying scrapers, dustbin bags etc. Tom has a fish-slice. Jack is carrying a bag of newspapers

Tom crosses and picks up the fallen statue at the top of the steps

Tom If we scrape all the muck away from the steps and get this standing again we could get it working.
Jack Where would you get the water?
Tom It used to be a fountain. There must be water somewhere.
William Cut off years ago. If that's broken off- (*indicating the statue*) the pipe must be blocked off. Or wrenched out.
Tom It would be great to have a fountain.
Jack You always go too far! Anyway that's not what they meant when they said let's clear up. They meant all the rubbish. I don't think Mrs Osbourne would let us muck about with a fountain.
Tom But that's why we're here early. You agreed —
Jack No I didn't. I came here early to get started – surprise the others. We could clean the steps —
Tom That's boring.
Jack Look, I haven't got much time. I've still got my paper round—

Tom and Jack begin in a rather half-hearted way to pick up some of the rubbish scattered around the fountain and stuff it into the black bags

William begins to scrape the steps to remove the encrusted filth

After a moment Jack stops and stares round. He sits on the edge of the pool lost in thought

William If we scrubbed these steps as well they'd look quite good. Come on, Tom!.
Tom (*messing about with the statue*) We've still got to get this standing up again. Even if there's no water. (*He holds the statue in place*) And he dives into the pool! (*He makes as if to roll the statue down the steps*)
William Don't do that! You'll break it. Come on you two. I'm not going to do it all by myself. I thought you were going to clear all this up – not muck about!

Tom props the statue up in a standing position by leaning it against the platform

Tom joins William and they scape away at the steps

Tom It's a bit boring. Come on, Jack, don't just sit there.
Jack I was thinking —

Act I

William Well don't. Do some work!

Jack gets up and joins William and Tom

Jack What have you got there?

Tom (*holding up the fish-slice*) This? I couldn't find a scraper. I'll have to take it back before Mum gets up. She'll want it for Dad's breakfast. It's a bit bendy for this job though.

William, Tom and Jack carry on working in silence for a moment, all three intent on what they are doing.

An Old Lady enters very quietly from behind the temple. She is dressed in a long grey dress in a soft floating material, with a cream lace collar. She is wearing a large-brimmed straw hat which shades her face. She is leaning on a black, silver-topped stick and she stands silently watching the boys

Jack, William and Tom do not see her and carry on working and chattering

Jack It's really hard to get this stuff off isn't it?

Tom Stinks a bit —

William (*scraping away furiously*) It's been here ages. It's got bedded in. Aaah! There! Look at that! (*He succeeds in detaching a large chunk of moss and mud*)

Tom seizes the chunk of moss and mud, and throws it at Jack

Jack gets up, dropping his scraper and wipes the mess from his face and chest

Jack (*with his eyes tight shut*) Don't do that, you stupid – that went in my eyes!

William Stop messing about, Tom. I wish we hadn't told you. You wanted to come —

William and Tom stand wrangling on the steps

Jack sees the Old Lady. He freezes and then tries to attract William and Tom's attention to her

Jack (*urgently*) Hey! You two! Stop it! (*He jerks his head back towards the Old Lady*)

The Old Lady is still standing quite still

William and Tom look where Jack is gesturing and see her. They get up slowly and stand awkwardly, heads down – not exactly afraid, but ill-at-ease, and disconcerted by her silent presence.

Old Lady You're up very early.

Jack Yes, the gates aren't locked any more. . . We didn't know we weren't allowed —

Old Lady (*with a smile*) Oh you're allowed. Don't let me stop you. (*She moves down and looks at the fountain*) You're making a very good job of that.

William, Tom and Jack mutter awkward thanks
Old Lady Was it your idea to come and do this?
Tom and William look at Jack
Jack It was me. I thought it would be good to clear all this muck away.
Old Lady So early?
Jack I'm up this early anyway – to do my paper round.
William Yes, if we came later we'd get given all the boring jobs —
Jack We wanted to do the fountain ourselves.
Tom We want to make it work. With the statue.
Old Lady It used to work. A long time ago. And there were waterlilies on the pool.
William This place has been shut up for ages.
Tom People used to climb over the gates though. That's why it's such a mess.
Jack Till they put broken glass and spikes on the wall.
Old Lady (*half to herself*) So that no-one could get in. (*She suddenly puts her hand to her head and rubs her forehead and closes her eyes. Then, a little breathless, she sits on the wall at the edge of the pool.*)
Jack Are you all right?
Old Lady Yes, I'm quite all right. I usually walk along the riverside in the morning. You don't sleep at my age. And these summer mornings are so beautiful, with the mist on the ground. . . I've come too far this morning. . . You have to be careful not to overdo things when you're as old as I am! This was always a favourite place of mine. I'm glad it's been unlocked again. . . I didn't expect to see – (*she pauses, then with a grave smile*) workmen here! What are your names?
Jack I'm Jack. This is William.
Tom And I'm Tom.
To their embarrassment she gets up and gravely shakes hands with each of them in turn.
Old Lady How do you do. William... Tom... Jack?
Jack (*wiping his hands on his trousers*) Our hands are a bit dirty.
Old Lady That doesn't matter. My name is Flora.
Jack
Tom   } (*together*) Erm... Hallo. How do you do
William
Old Lady Perhaps we shall meet again.
Tom (*hastily*) I shouldn't think so.
Jack (*explaining Tom's apparent rudeness*) We were only going to come this once this early.
William Yes, just to clear the fountain and the steps.

The Old Lady does not respond

Jack (*impelled to speak by her silence*) We'll be back – with the others – during the day. I've got to do my paper round now. . . There'll be loads of us – during the day. *We* won't be back this early – I shouldn't think. . .

Act I

Jack stares, puzzled, at the Old Lady, who is looking at him with a kind of sad intensity

Tom We ought to be going now.
Old Lady Yes, of course, I mustn't keep you. (*She moves away and stands on the platform, watching them.*)

Very quickly and quietly William, Tom and Jack collect up their belongings and mutter goodbyes

Goodbye. (*She watches them go*)

Tom, William and Jack exit

There is a thread of wistful, dawn-like music as the lights slowly come up to a warm golden morning light

The Old Lady crosses to the fountain and touches the little statue propped up as Tom left it

The Old Lady looks round sadly and exits through the temple

The Lights are now full up and it is a brilliantly sunny day

15: Fancy Dress

Laura, Louise, Emma, Amy, Joanna, Abby, Sue, William, Mark, Michael, Tom, Jack and Chris enters, led by Danny

Katie and David drag on a skip full of costumes

The Company dispose themselves about the stage in groups

Jack has a guitar

Some members of the company have books, bags etc

Laura flops down and stretches out on the grass

Louise produces a bottle of lemonade and she, Abby and Sue take a swig

Each group is self contained and absorbed in its own conversations, but aware of what is going on generally

Laura Oh, it's too hot.

Emma fans Laura vigorously

Laura Oh lovely.
Amy (*stretching out*) No it's not. It's gorgeous. I'd like to stay here for ever. I'm getting to like this place. Specially now Hilary's fixed the weather for us.
Louise She's ordered some hailstorms for when Greshams start their campaign.

Emma begins to fan herself

Laura Don't stop.

Emma You should have brought your own.
Laura It's a shame we're only here in the evenings, except for Sundays. I don't want to go to work tomorrow. I want to stay here all day and get brown.
Danny We ought to put our own padlock on that gate.
Chris Why?
Danny Keep other people out.
Joanna Very public spirited.
Danny Anybody could get in and nick all our stuff. Or smash it up.
Chris We're not going to leave anything here overnight.
Danny No, but we're not going to stop here all day either, are we?
David We can't lock the place up – not on our own.
Danny Once we've moved in here we're stuck, aren't we?
Katie Oh don't worry. There'll always be somebody when the stuff's here – I don't mind stopping —
Danny I think it's mad rehearsing here anyway. You'll have all those old biddies from the Over Nineties club wandering in, "Oh – doin' a play are you? Ooooh, What's it about?" And kids chucking bottles.
David You can set the old biddies on beating up the kids. They'd love that.
Katie If we always shut the gate people won't realise they're allowed in as well. They'll think it's just us. Anyway, I think it's nice having people watching – they'll want to come and see the show.
David Not if they've seen our rehearsals they won't.
Danny Don't be nasty, you'll make Katie cry. Always likes to see the best in everything, don't you Katie? Except me.
David You're not Nick though are you? (*Quickly before Katie can respond*) Talking of rehearsals, what exactly are we going to rehearse? I see no play.
Amy (*drily*) It'll probably be a monologue by Sophie. With us standing round applauding.
Mark I thought Sophie wasn't going to bother with this one.
Danny So did Katie, didn't you?. . . But Nick's very persuasive. . . Isn't he Katie?
Amy (*drily*) Oh, Sophie's not doing much this time. She's just going to research the story, tell Nick what to write, help Charlotte direct it and play the lead. She'll probably rig the lights and sell programmes as well if you ask her nicely. She didn't want to let us down! She knows how useless we are without her.
Sue She can do the props if she likes.
Amy Not glamorous enough!
Katie (*changing the subject and crossing to the skip*) Amy, Laura, we ought to sort all this out.
Amy Oh can't it wait till Nick and Charlotte get here?
Katie Well, I think Nick will want to talk about the play.
Emma I thought you were supposed to be helping with the research.
Katie – I have —
Emma Has Sophie taken that over as well?
Katie She was always going to — (*She bites her lip and looks away*)

Laura silently chides Emma for her lack of tact

Act I

Danny (*crossing to the skip and flinging it open*) Yeuerrch!!! What a stink. Where do you get all this?

Amy glances into the skip and wrinkles her nose in disgust

Amy Mothballs! Hilary got hold of it from somewhere...
Louise Some play is probably about to go on stage minus its costumes.
Michael Hilary may have got them. It was me who had to drive nearly to Reading to collect them! My van won't do more that ten miles without a transplant.
David Why couldn't she go? (*He pulls out an outrageous beaded dress from the skip*)
Michael (*shrugging*) Meeting or something.
Danny (*holding the dress against himself*) No, this is hers. This is what she slips into at home for a quiet dinner *à deux*!

David joins Danny and takes out another slinky number. He holds it against himself and pouts

David Or a ménage à trois!

The other gather round the skip and begin to pull out a varied assortment of costumes, masks, swords, boxing gloves etc

Katie Oh dear! She said there were lots of things we could use —
Amy This is just jumble.

16: When You've Got the Frock (Music IX)

By the time the song ends everyone is half-dressed in a motley assortment of costumes – mainly eighteenth century but with bizarre additions

Mark (*speaking*)	No it isn't...
(*Singing*)	Think of the characters lying
	Hidden at the bottom of the pile.
	Think of the dresses sighing
	For the chance to become a girl.
	Think of the frock-coats waiting
	To grace a manly hip.
	All those people that need creating
	Waiting their chance in a theatrical skip.
Chorus	Put on the clothes, let out the people,
	Get out the costumes and let them live.
	Frock coat
	Lace cuff
	Hat like a steeple
	Corsets
	Camisoles
	Boots that won't give.
	Hook nose, earrings, watch chain and bins
	Get the outside right, watch the inside grow

| | This is where the magic begins
When you've got the frock, you've got the show! |
|---|---|
| **Amy** | Give me a good pair of stockings,
Give me the right pair of shoes
Good quality suitings and frockings
And there's no way that I can lose.
When the lipstick shade is spot on
And the hair's just right for the part
From then on I will be red hot on
Finding the truth in my theatrical art. |
| **Chorus** | Put on the clothes, let out the people,
Get out the costumes and let them live.
Frock coat
Lace cuff
Hat like a steeple
Corsets
Camisoles
Boots that won't give.
Hook nose, earrings, watch chain and bins
Get the outside right, watch the inside grow
This is where the magic begins
When you've got the frock, you've got the show! |
| **Laura** | Rush in and slip off the raincoat,
Seven-oh-five and I'm late;
Flustered and worried again, throat
Aching, and face like a plate.
Put on the slap and the clobber
And something calms all the strife:
Take a look in the dressing room mirror
A theatrical costume coming to life! |
| **Chorus** | Put on the clothes, let out the people,
Get out the costumes and let them live.
Frock coat
Lace cuff
Hat like a steeple
Corsets
Camisoles
Boots that won't give.
Hook nose, earrings, watch chain and bins
Get the outside right, watch the inside grow
This is where the magic begins
When you've got the frock, you've got the show! |

Nick, Sophie and Charlotte enter with files, notebooks etc.

Act I

17: Storytime

Charlotte (*looking round dispiritedly*) These the famous costumes?
Amy 'Fraid so.
Charlotte Oh well, don't say I didn't warn you. Where is Madam?
Amy Don't know. Haven't seen her for a couple of days.
Charlotte She's probably lost interest in us by now. She was getting a bit lustful about the new bypass last week.
Nick All right, now listen everybody, we've got our play – well sort of —
Charlotte What we've actually got is a story – a true story – that really happened. Here. We can talk about it – improvise, whatever you like, decide what we want to do, then Nick can go away and write it.
David Oh, do we have to? I thought we were going to do a proper play. I'm not learning a different set of lines each rehearsal.
Laura Make a change for you learn any.
Amy And we want something that uses these costumes. We can't afford to hire any and I'm not making any this year.

Louise, Laura and Amy take some costumes out of the skip. They are basically eighteenth century but with some aberrations

Nick Sophie – you've got all the background.
Sophie (*consulting her notes*) Once upon a time – there was a huge house here with massive grounds all over this area. It was built in seventeen thirty-seven by Sir Joshua Freshwater. He was the second baronet. His father William Freshwater was a down-to-earth sort of man from Leicestershire somewhere and he made loads of money from silks and things – and he did the King some sort of favour. So the King gave him a title and some land... Joshua was his eldest son. William built a Town House. That was pulled down in – (*she consults her notes*) eighteen eighty-four. But Joshua spent all his time here. He got artists and composers and poets and they had loads of entertainments – music, plays, poetry readings, dances – all these temples were used – there were nine of them then —
Danny Sounds a load of laughs. That ought to pack 'em in!
Sophie You don't put that in the play. It's just background.
Danny (*stretching out on the ground*) Wake me up when you get to the bodice-ripping.
Sophie All right Danny, sorry if it's too much for you!
Danny Carry on. You've done all this research and you're going to tell us more than we want to know about the Freshwaters.
Amy (*finding an elegant brocade coat*) Hey look this isn't bad.

Danny sits up and puts on the brocade coat

Sophie Joshua was a bit of a snob —
Nick You don't know that. There's nothing in the records. You just took against him —

Sophie with a murderous look hands Nick her notes

Nick declines and sits down prepared to remain quiet

Sophie He was a snob and wanted to get in with the aristocracy and forget that all his money had come from trade. He used to hold fantastic parties here —
Laura Masked balls! With highwaymen and a mysterious cloaked lady whose secret is discovered at midnight when she takes off her mask and reveals...

Laura seizes Joanna and puts a jewelled mask and cloak on her. They throw themselves into their improvisations with energetic enjoyment and great skill, but there is an underlying hint of malice and a desire to put Sophie off her stride

Sophie is aware of this and tries to ride it out, but she is disconcerted and a little hurt

Nick is also aware and is angered by it, and tries to help her out. His easy popularity contrasts with Sophie's inability to win the group over

Charlotte watches sardonically

Sophie *(ploughing on)* He only had one daughter —
Danny Get out, girl, and never darken my doors again. I, Sir Joshua, have spoken. You have brought shame and disgrace to my white hairs!
Joanna No, dearest Father, I beg you, let me stay. I have done no wrong.
Sophie Shut up! As he had no sons he brought her up as if she'd been a boy —
Mark Hey Joanna! Over here!

Mark runs up and bowls an imaginary ball at Joanna who takes guard

Danny Come on, girl get your left foot across!
Sophie She was taught Greek, Latin, poetry, music, painting. The lot in fact —
Nick — An artistic education. Sir Josh wasn't into huntin', shootin' and fishin'. So by the time she was seventeen she was the equal of any man —
Sophie — the superior actually! But that didn't alter the fact that if she married, everything would belong to her husband and she wouldn't be able to touch it. That was the law then. And if she didn't marry it would all go out of the family anyway. Her dad was obsessed with this place by then and she went along with it.
Danny You're a hell of a gel, but why aren't you a boy – solve all me problems.
Joanna Oh dear Papa, forgive me – forgive me for being a weak and feeble female.
Louise *(disgusted)* Oh come on!
Sophie Eventually – and she *agreed* – her father married her off to a distant cousin. Probably because his name was Freshwater – just to keep the name going. But Sir Josh thought up this brilliant wheeze. He gambled on his daughter having a son and he made this Will. Everything was entailed or something – Held in Trust for the boys so that when she died everything was

Act I

to go straight to her sons, missing out the husband. He couldn't touch it at all. He was the pits. Didn't have any money of his own —
Nick Behaved himself till dad died then set about drinking and gambling away all the money —
Danny No *that's* my part!... Come here me proud beauty, do as I bid ye or you'll feel my riding crop across your shoulders.
Joanna You may beat me but you will never break my spirit! (*She gestures to the others who applaud and cheer*)
Charlotte I'm beginning to think we should do 'Charley's Aunt'
Sophie Sit down Danny, we'll let you know. (*Firmly*) She was of course, very unhappy. Her marriage was a disaster.

Joanna adopts a sorrowing pose

After her Father died her sons were her whole life —
David Eh?
Sophie She had three sons.
David Oh?
Sophie (*impatiently*) She stayed *here* all the time, while her husband was in the Town House —
David *After* the three sons, I presume.

The others, apart from Sophie, laugh

Sophie (*coldly, cutting across the laughter*) Trying to keep this place as her father wanted it. She actually saw to the building of some of these temples —
Katie There was a young architect and painter. They became very friendly —
Mark Oh yeah?
Katie But he went away before the building was finished
Danny Cowboy!
Sophie Then her husband started to bring all his drunken gambling cronies here —
Nick And they started smashing up the place —
Katie He treated her appallingly – beat her.
Danny I definitely see myself in this part.
Charlotte Are you sure? It is an acting part.

Danny rifles through the skip and finds a whip

Katie She couldn't take much more.
Danny Come here wench! Clean me boots or I'll thrash ye! (*He cracks the whip; quietly*) "A woman, a dog and a walnut tree, The more you beat them the better they be." (*He stares rather unpleasantly at Katie*)

There is a slight uneasy pause

Katie lowers her eyes and slips away from Danny

Emma, who has been watching them, moves forward decisively

Emma Right! That's it!. This story is *out*!
Danny What did I say?

Laura (*increasingly disappointed with the contents of the skip*) This is a load of rubbish!.

The others, apart from Sophie, laugh

No, I mean these – honestly. (*She darts a malicious glance at Sophie, nevertheless*)

Amy No, there's quite a few things here we could tart up. Depends what we need.

Katie joins Laura, Louise and Amy and they take the last costumes out of the skip

Nick (*to Danny; removing the whip from him*) Keep your fantasies to yourself will you?

Charlotte This is a waste of time. Let's decide on a real play and get on with it – or pull out all together.

Nick Suits me.

Sophie Oh no! After all this work. It's giving up —

Nick And you never give up.

Katie Look at this. (*Very carefully she reaches into the skip and pulls out something carefully wrapped in tissue paper*)

Katie and Amy unwrap and hold up an eighteenth century dress

It is very beautiful, cream and gold with pearls sewn onto it. Katie holds it against herself

Laura Isn't it gorgeous!

Amy It doesn't look as if it's even been worn.

Louise I wonder what it was for.

Katie Pearls – for tears.

There is a momentary silence as the rest of them look at the dress. They are all quite still

Nick (*quietly*) Put it on, Sophie.

Sophie Me? I'd never get into that —

Amy (*acidly under her breath*) Yes you would. It's bigger than it looks.

Sophie – I don't think. I don't like to.

Katie (*almost throwing at her*) Why not? It's only a costume. Look, it's got a zip up the back. That cream satin is polyester. Come round the back of the temple. I'll help you put it on.

There is an awkward pause

Sophie shrugs and exits with Katie through the temple

Amy watches them go. Then exchanges glances with Laura

Amy (*crossing back to the skip; briskly*) Don't leave all this stuff all over the ground, it'll get filthy.

Everyone begins to put the costumes etc. back into the skip

Mrs Weekly and Mrs Pagett enter with refreshments and a rug, and make their way to the platform. They tut-tut over the mess

Act I

David with a flourish gestures for them to sit on the bench

Mrs Pagett and Mrs Weekly sit on the bench and watch the proceedings with interest, drinking tea and eating biscuits

Mrs Pagett Thought you were supposed to be tidying this place up not bringing more rubbish in.

Liz, a reporter and Gary, a photographer, enter. Liz has a small portable tape recorder; Gary a camera. Liz is brisk and efficient. Gary mooches around as if he would rather be elsewhere

Liz Well, this seems to be the place all right. Who's in charge?
Charlotte Why?
Liz We're from *The Chronicle*. I'm Liz Mackie. That's Gary. We have a big local interest story about to break here I gather.
Nick Did Mrs Osbourne send you?
Liz Hang on, I've got the name somewhere. My editor tells me to go and I go. It *was* a woman who phoned...
Nick Well, we're the Foreground Theatre Company, Mrs Osbourne is – (*thinking furiously*) our – er – business manager and we're performing a play here as part of the campaign to save the park, which Mrs Osbourne also —
Liz (*dismissively*) Yes, yes, we got all that last week. What's this photo opportunity?
Danny Me?
Liz (*drily*) Yes, Lovely. Ah, here we are. (*She fishes a piece of paper out of her bag*) Which of you is Zoë Dean?

All the girls shake their heads

Charlotte Never heard of her. Not one of ours. Sure you've come to the right place?

Liz is irritated but she is used to other people's inefficiency

Liz Right! Well, I don't know what you're supposed to do here, Gary.
Gary Uh?
Liz Go back to sleep. (*Looking round*) We've got pictures of this dump from all angles already. (*To Charlotte*) What can you tell me that I don't know?
Charlotte (*drily*) You're the ace reporter. What do you want to know?
Liz They warned me there'd by days like this! (*Patiently*) What play are you doing?
David Good question.
Nick It's not written yet.
Liz Well, that's different, I suppose. Sold any tickets yet?
Nick Otherwise we're cast and ready to go. The big local story happened here in seventeen sixty-two —

Sophie enters a little self-consciously from behind the temple, followed by Katie. She looks stunningly beautiful in the low-cut cream and gold dress

Everyone turns to look at Sophie. They all stay still and look at her for a moment

Nick (*softly*) That's great, Sophie.
Katie (*wistfully*) Do you like it, Nick?
Laura (*touching the dress*) It's beautiful.
Mrs Weekly It's very nice, dear.
Mrs Pagett Lovely material! And all those pearls!
Nick (*improvising like mad*) There's your picture. This is Sophie. She's playing the heroine of our play, Flora. This is Danny, the wicked Captain Harry Freshwater, and these are her tragic little sons.

Nick gestures for Jack, Tom and William to come forward

Jack, Tom and William cross and sit by the fountain

Danny adopts a pose, watching them

Sophie crosses and stands with Jack, Tom and William

Gary moves around photographing them and Liz switches on her tape recorder

Hilary enters and stops to watch what is happening

Nick moves to greet Hilary

The Lights fade slightly except on the central tableau by the fountain

Nick has found his play

The whole group stand silent, entering into Nick's mood

(*Gesturing to Hilary*) Shh! Go on Sophie.

18: Leaving (Music X)

Sophie (singing) Leaving,
Stealing away,
Leaving,
No other way to
Save them,
My little sons,
Sleeping,
What mother runs off
Leaving,
Stealing away,
Leaving
You alone.

The Chorus repeats the first verse, very softly, while Sophie sings the second verse to Nick's counter-melody

Chorus	Leaving,	Sophie	Leaving,
	Stealing away,		Breaking my heart,
	Leaving,		Leaving,
	No other way to		Living apart now,
	Save them,		Crying,

Act I

    My little sons,   Hiding my tears,
    Sleeping,   Trying
    What mother runs off   To stifle my fears that
    Leaving,   Leaving
    Stealing away,   Is breaking my heart,
    Leaving   Leaving
    You alone.   You alone.

19: Mr Freshwater

Mr Whittaker enters DS with Zoë Dean. He looks extremely pleased with himself

Mr Freshwater enters diffidently behind them and looks round with interest

Sophie sees them and stops

Mr Whittaker Oh please don't stop. That was charming. Good-afternoon, Mrs Osbourne.
Hilary Hallo.
Mr Whittaker You know my assistant, of course. Zoë Dean...
Hilary
Zoë *(together)* How do you do
Mr Whittaker What a hive of activity. How's it going?

The activity has, of course, stopped

Nick Fine.
Mr Whittaker Well, I hope it's a great success. I'm looking forward to it immensely – as I'm sure this gentleman is... May I introduce – Mr George Freshwater.

There is amazement as they look at George. There is a babble of noise. Some are interested in a real live Freshwater, while others are suspicious

George is rather embarrassed

Hilary stares at the self-satisfied Whittaker in horror

Gary mooches about waiting to be told what to do

Liz *(realising that this is her story)* Well, well, well. Now this might be something! Action, Gary!
Mr Whittaker *(silkily)* Mr Freshwater – as you must have gathered – is a descendant of the gentleman who built this house. The heir to what's left of the Freshwater Inheritance.
Hilary *(faintly)* Are – are you the owner of the park then?
George I suppose I must be.

There is silence

Mr Whittaker Mr Freshwater lives in Lincolnshire. He had no idea he had – interests here. You can imagine how surprised he was when we tracked him down. It's all thanks to Zoë's marvellous detective work!

Zoë Thank you, Giles. It was fun, actually!
Hilary (*drily*) I'm sure it was.
Mr Whittaker This, sadly, is all that's left of the estate, Mr Freshwater – but as you can see – it's a charming site.

Mr Whittaker leads George through the group, who stare at him resentfully, up to the temple

George smiles worriedly at Sophie

    Your great-great – I don't know how many greats – grandmother I presume.

Sophie stares stonily at him

    The other piece of news is that Mr Freshwater has agreed to sell the land to Gresham Developments.

There is total silence.

George It – It's no use to me you see!

There is general consternation; Sophie, Nick and Charlotte do not move

Danny tears off his coat and throws it into the skip

Nick You'd better take that off, Sophie. We won't be needing it now.
Mr Whittaker Oh, no, no. You don't understand. We don't want to stop your show. Mr Freshwater, I'm sure, will be thrilled to see the story of his ancestors.
Nick (*white with fury*) Oh yes, I'm sure he would. But what if we don't want to go on? What's the point? We're not doing this for your benefit. You're not going to use us as cheap publicity for your stinking schemes!
Hilary No, Nick! Calm down. We've got to do the play. We've committed ourselves and we can't go back on that. We've got a great many V.I.P.s coming. You can't pull out now.
Nick But it'll look like we're launching *them*!!

There is uproar

Hilary No, it won't. The fight's not over yet. You don't give up at the first setback. Mr Whittaker hasn't heard the last of us!
Mr Whittaker I do admire you, Mrs Osbourne, but why don't you admit defeat – this once?
Hilary Never!

The Old Lady enters from behind the temple as the song begins. No-one sees her and she stands leaning on her stick silently watching what is going on

                20: Get the Picture – Finale (Music XI)

Gary and Liz   1. Get the picture
                             There's the story

Act I   37

>   Forget the actors
>   The drama's here.
>
>   Face the camera
>   Good and smiley
>   The crucial fact is
>   They've found the heir.

Zoë, Mr Whittaker,   2. We'll get into the picture
and Mr Freshwater   We'll smile a lot and shake hands.
                                    The broad smile of the winner
                                    Is the photograph everyone understands.

>   We're not used to losing
>   And we don't intend to stop
>   Seizing our chances, and being
>   The people who come out on top.

Verses 1 and 2 are sung together

Hilary (*solo*)   3. Oh, don't be downhearted
                                    We're certainly not beaten yet.
                                    This little game has hardly started
                                    We've only lost the first set.
                                    This is no more than a setback.
                                    We'll stare these new facts in the face
                                    And we won't give up till we get back
                                    Our park as everyone's place.

Mrs Pagett and Mrs Weekly sing in duet while the chorus sings a counter-melody to "La la la"

Mrs Pagett } (*together*)   4. Why do people change things?
Mrs Weekly
Mrs Weekly   Do you know?
Mrs Pagett   No.
Mrs Weekly   Nor I.
Mrs Pagett } (*together*)   The old park, Sunday evenings
Mrs Weekly   Was more than money could buy.
                                    You could stroll and listen
Mrs Pagett   Remember?
Mrs Weekly   Yes.
Mrs Pagett   It was nice.
Mrs Weekly } (*together*)   The deck-chairs, the band from the Mission.
Mrs Pagett   Changes always mean worse.

The Chorus sings in unison

Chorus   5. What's the point of doing our play
                                    If the park's already sold?
                                    There's nothing to celebrate today

Except the power of Whittaker's gold.
We don't need telling that power
Usually gets its way
And there's more than one kind of shower
Can wash out the best kind of play.

Verses one, two, three, four and five are sung together in counterpoint

At the climax Zoë, Gary, Liz, Mr Whittaker and Mr Freshwater exit

The Chorus breaks into two groups which sing in harmony and canon

Chorus Maybe we are beaten
Maybe the park is dead
Maybe we are beaten
Maybe the park is dead
Maybe we are beaten
Maybe the park is dead
Maybe we are beaten
Maybe the park is dead
When the voice of money has spoken
There's nothing more to be said.
When the voice of money has spoken
There's nothing more to be said.

Maybe the dream is over
Maybe the spirits are gone
Maybe the dream is over
Maybe the spirits are gone
Maybe the dream is over
Maybe the spirits are gone
Maybe the dream is over
Maybe the spirits are gone
But for us, this is our theatre
And somehow the show must go on.
But for us, this is our theatre
And somehow the show must go on.

Everyone exits excitedly, apart from Katie, in all directions

The Old Lady stands silently, watching them leave

Katie stands alone, watching her

Lights fade

ACT II

21: Minuet (Music XII)

The same. Late afternoon

The curtain rises on a transformed scene. The rubbish has gone and the old mattress has been removed. The graffiti has been scrubbed clean from the stonework. A string of coloured lights has been fixed across the top of the temple. There is a huge full 'moon' in the sky

A minuet is playing and is being danced by Sophie, Nick, Mark, Joanna, Michael and Emma. All are dressed in eighteenth century costume.

Charlotte sits watching DS out of the way. She has her 'director' clutter with her, such as her lighting notes, her clipboard and script, etc

Sue is beside Charlotte and as stage manager is hung about with marking tapes and all the paraphernalia required for a technical rehearsal

The dance ends and everyone applauds politely

Mark, Joanna, Michael and Emma exit, quietly talking

Nick breaks away abruptly, DS of the fountain

Sophie glances round anxiously then moves across to him

The music continues very softly

22: Flora's Temple

Sophie Don't you care for our company, Mr Hervey?
Nick (*evenly*) Not all of it – no.
Sophie I'm sorry. It is not – entirely – of my choosing.
Nick And it is not my place to criticize Captain Freshwater. And his friends. But after what was said to me tonight... So let me slip away quietly. No-one will miss me —

There is a burst of raucous laughter from off stage

Sophie looks across anxiously to the place it comes from

    I could not promise to keep my temper if any more insults were offered to me. Or to you.
Sophie I should have – oh this was all to have been so different. (*Petulantly*) Why did Harry and his rabble of friends have to come here tonight of all nights?

Act II

Nick turns away

It was to have been – a magical evening. Harry isn't interested in our temples! He only comes here to make sure that I am miserable...
Nick It is your husband's house. He pays my bills.
Sophie With my money!
Nick He can do as he pleases. I have built what you wanted, but he has the right to tear it all down. And you cannot stop him.
Sophie Don't! *(She looks round sadly)* The Dedication of Flora's Temple! With music and flowers. Don't tell him. Don't tell anyone about that. Let him think it's just somewhere for him to sit and kick the mud off his boots!
Nick Flora – Whatever happens it *is* a temple to Flora. I know, I am its architect and whatever happens every stone was put in place for that reason alone.

Nick leads Sophie into the temple then steps away DS

Sophie Edmund —
Nick No, don't move. Stay in your Temple... Now it's finished I must go...

Song 23: Where Flora Walks (Music XIII)

(Singing)   Where Flora walks, the flowers spring;
Fresh blossoms from her lips she breathes.
To all her children she bequeaths
The gift of beauty, joy of song.
Raise then her temple in this grove,
And may her worship never cease;
May all her followers find peace
And the joy of everlasting love.

Her gentle presence lingers still
Her shade still glides beneath these trees,
And faint upon the sighing breeze
Her singing, like a distant bell
Swells and recedes, is heard, then lost.
And sometimes on a summer night
When the moon is low and the stars are bright
Her gentle ghost glides slowly past.

Where Flora walks, the flowers spring;
Fresh blossoms from her lips she breathes.
To all her children she bequeaths
The gift of beauty, joy of song... *(Before the verse ends he shatters the mood)* And so on. OK?

24: Technical

Charlotte moves US and shading her eyes stares up at the lights

Charlotte Yeah, fine. Everybody on stage, please.

The group enters, chattering:

Michael and David drag on the costume skip. Michael is wearing modern dress and carrying his eighteenth century jacket, carefully folded. David is wearing his own jeans or shorts and a voluminous eighteenth century shirt and brocade waistcoat over them

Amy follows and takes a pile of plastic costume bags from the skip and begins to hand them round to the cast

Kate, Emma, Laura, Louise, Jack, William, Tom and Chris enter, all wearing modern dress

Mark, Abby and Joanna are all in full eighteenth century costume

Chris, can I have another look at the daylight state? Tom, kill the moon. All right everybody, listen please.

The group continues to talk

Charlotte Listen! You can get out of those clothes now.

Joanna, Abby and Jack exit

The moon goes out and the stage is flooded with brilliant light

Tom crosses the stage carrying the moon, an unromantic circle of gauze or plastic now it is unlit. He looks reproachfully at Charlotte as he exits with the moon

There is now a warm, gold, late afternoon light on the central area, but it is getting dark outside the pool of light

The group begin to take plastic bags from Amy, and drop jackets, hats etc into the skip

Amy *Please* put your costumes in the plastic bags. Don't just dump them in the skip.

Charlotte Right, that's it for tonight. Thank you everybody. Six o'clock tomorrow Sophie, Jack, Katie, Louise, Danny and Abby. The rest of you seven fifteen sharp. Don't be late.

The group breaks up and begins to drift away. Amy, Katie, Laura and Emma sit in the temple

Chris unhooks the fairy lights and drops them centre stage

Chris exits with Tom and William

Sophie exits abruptly after a glance at Nick

Nick and Charlotte confer over a technical schedule

Louise picks up a large cardboard box full of handbills, programmes and publicity material from one of the benches and begins to look through the

Act II

contents with mounting irritation

Everyone seems drained of all energy and there is an undercurrent of dispirited irritability

Louise When's Mrs Osbourne going to be here again?
Charlotte (*evenly*) She's in Crete.
Louise Oh.
Charlotte For another ten days.
Louise Only – she was supposed to be doing publicity.
Charlotte I know.
Michael And she was supposed to be organizing the seating.
Charlotte I know.
Michael Dave, Chris and me – we can't do that. We've got enough to do.
Charlotte I know
David Who's going to do it all then?
Charlotte I don't know, I'm just the director of this farce.
Nick Thank you Charlotte. I thought I'd written a poignant little tragedy – with warm-hearted overtones, and a few jokes.
Charlotte Oh for God's sake Nick, if you can't say anything useful shut up! I've got enough to do.
Nick I told you it was a bloody waste of time. After the oil slick produced that pathetic little wimp like a rabbit out of a hat, it was all over bar the shouting. There's no point in any of us doing any of this. Not now. So we might as well get it over with and get the hell out of it.
Charlotte You know that and I know that but what about Hilary Good-Causes-Unlimited Osbourne. Drops us in it and bogs off to Crete.
Katie She wouldn't have been much use if she'd stayed. She was terribly upset – she just seemed to collapse and give in —
David So she has to have a holiday to get over it.
Mark All together now – Aaah!.
David I never thought she could be so wet. Not even being here when the balloon goes up... All right if I get out of this clobber? (*He indicates the few elements of eighteenth century costume he is wearing*)

Charlotte nods

David exits

Charlotte Well, it's a pointless waste of time doing the show – we all know that – but we're in too far to get out.
Amy We were always going to do a show. It's just not – for anything now. I mean, except itself.
Louise Art for art's sake.
Emma Well, it'll be a "Goodbye to the Park", I suppose. We didn't know it was here. We didn't know anything about it. Now we do. And in six months it will all be gone.
Nick And we'll be the funeral service! – I could strangle Hilary Osbourne with my bare hands!
Charlotte Not if I get to her first you couldn't.

Joanna enters, wearing modern dress

Laura Oh come on, I can't stand all this gloom. We haven't lost anything. We were going to do a play anyway. We're doing a play. And we're doing our own show which we've never done before.

Nick (*cliché voice*) Oh yes, look on the bright side that's what I always say! (*Savagely*) I just don't like being made a fool of that's all. I'm not into good causes and I'm sure as hell not getting involved again. I wouldn't be doing this gripping little historical pageant if it wasn't for Hilary. First sign of trouble and she's off. Got about as much fight in her as our budgie! And bloody Sophie nags me into writing it because she likes pushing people around, not to mention poncing about herself, in a nice frock. It would have been better all round if Captain Freshwater had strangled his precious wife and built a blacking factory here! We've got to get up there and smile and do the damn show because we've sold lots of tickets and the Mayor's coming. What for? Is Whittaker going to get up at the end of the show and say, "Thanks for all the publicity folks, the bulldozers are in tomorrow." Or do we all wear black armbands and have a minute's silence and chuck wreaths in the river?

Louise I don't think any of that matters.

Nick is incredulous

But I don't think she should have left us to do all the work.

Nick Thanks very much.

Laura Don't go on Nick. We haven't lost anything actually – except the chance of doing *Guys and Dolls* in the Church Hall.

Joanna Everybody knows why we're here. We can just smile bravely in defeat and collect our Brownie points for being good citizens. We don't need Mrs Osbourne.

Mark Oh, she'll be here on the last night taking all the credit —

Nick I wouldn't bank on it – she's probably up to her neck in a "Save the Minotaur" campaign at this very moment. We should never have listened to her in the first place. And don't say "I told you so", Charlotte, or I'll garrotte you.

Charlotte I wouldn't dream of it. I did though, didn't I? It's not my fault if you always take the easy way out, Nick.

Nick Me?

Charlotte Yes, it was easier to say yes to Hilary than no wasn't it?

Nick I see. Great. It's all my fault. Right. Thanks very much.

Katie Oh for God's sake stop whingeing, Nick!

The others look at Katie in amazement

Whoever said it was going to be easy? Hilary runs away and you go throwing tantrums. Where's the difference? *You've* got plenty out of this only you're to stupid to see it. Laura's right. What have we lost? So, we're not going to be all over the papers with, "Local Theatre Group saves park from greedy developers." We're still doing a play – which is all we were going to do in the first place! We weren't exactly exerting ourselves were we? We've had a go at – oh – getting involved and it hasn't worked. So we won't do that again.

Act II

But what's the point of spoiling what we *are* doing, moaning all the time and getting at each other. You make me sick! Now you've got me doing it!!

Katie exits

There is a pause

Nick exits, after Katie

Amy Don't chuck yourself in the river! You'll ruin your costume!
Laura Come on, Emma, what have you done with your frock?

Emma and Laura exit behind the temple

Michael Do you want these lights in the trees tomorrow? (*He indicates the tangled pile of fairy lights*)
Charlotte No, don't bother, I've seen them working, that'll do. I'll be back about five.

David enters with a pile of costumes

David Mine. Dan's and Joanna's. See you in the pub.
Mark Wait for me...

David drops the costumes in the skip and exits whistling, followed by Mark

Michael sits on the edge of the fountain, patiently untangling the lights

Amy Don't just dump them —
Sue (*shouting off stage after David*) Please put your props on the prop table, or I shall turn very nasty!
Charlotte (*wistfully*) I could have done a lovely production of *A Midsummer Night's Dream*. Or *No Sex Please, We're British*. Good night – I may or may not be back.

Charlotte exits

Amy I won't be long.
Michael Don't worry, I'm not in a hurry. I'll bring the van round to the gate when you've got all the costumes.
Amy Thanks.
Michael That's all right.

Emma and Laura enter. Emma is carrying her costume. She folds it and drops it into the skip.

Amy Thanks. Has Nick gone home in his costume?
Laura Dunno. He's had a shock. I don't think he could believe the worm had finally turned.
Louise Katie actually criticizing him? About time. That's another first for this show.
Michael One day Nick is going to realize Katie is much nicer than Sophie.

Amy, Laura and Louise look at Michael with amused surprise

Clever people like Nick don't rate niceness though.
Louise Well, he'd better hurry up. This is *La* Sophe's farewell performance.
Emma Oh, it's depressing isn't it?
Laura What Sophie leaving? I can bear it!
Amy *If* she goes. She's been threatening to for long enough. I'll believe it when I see it.
Laura Shame. I'd quite like to see Katie have a go at playing Flora.
Louise Oh Sophie won't go anywhere before the last night.
Amy I must say getting Katie to understudy Sophie is the *nicest* thing Nick's managed yet!
Laura Just in case Sophie does a runner.
Louise It wouldn't have hurt him to write something decent for Katie. She was dying to be in this one...
Emma Oh don't go on! I was depressed enough already!
Amy There's a surprise.
Emma We're not going to get this show on, are we? Nick hasn't even finished it yet – not properly. David doesn't know his lines. Danny's never here. It's bound to rain... All this effort for nothing.
Laura You always say that!
Amy Everybody's tired.
Louise It has all gone wrong though. It would be different if we hadn't got all involved in the first place.
Emma Yes – we're a failure before we've even started.
Amy Well, we won't make this mistake again. If you don't want to get let down don't bother with anybody else.
Michael Are you going to be much longer?
Amy Just need Nick's costume. Sorry.
Louise What about you, Michael, are you depressed?
Michael Nope. I never get involved anyway. I just fit in where I'm wanted. I don't even read the plays.
Louise Why not?
Michael Don't like plays much. I just do it for the company.
Amy One of these days you might just get more than you bargained for...

25: It'll Probably End in Tears (Music XIV)

Amy	Don't get involved.
Emma	People are the trouble
Louise	Don't waste your time
Laura	Brickbats and jeers.
Michael	You were hoping for a house, and all you get is rubble
All	It'll probably end in tears.
Emma	When you want some help
Louise	Everyone starts running.
Laura	Ask for commitment
Michael	The crowd disappears.
Amy	Your show will be wonderful, marvellous and stunning
All	It'll probably end in tears.

Act II

Louise	And now there's the park
Laura	Really worth saving
Michael	A gift handed down to us
Amy	For hundreds of years.
Emma	We take on the money-men, we know we must be raving
All	It'll probably end in tears.
Laura	Why not stay at home?
Michael	Never leave your bedroom
Amy	Pull all the blinds down
Emma	Be one of the drears.
Louise	Never lift your head up, unless you're sure there's headroom
All	It'll certainly end in tears.

Louise, Laura, Michael, Emma and Amy perfrom a brief dance break, the length of one verse of the song.

All	So what do we do?
	Do we keep on going?
	Do we give it everything
	In spite of our fears?
	With our eyes wide open, we carry on rehearsing
	It'll probably end, it'll probably end,
	It'll probably
	Usually
	Certainly
	Definitely
	And unquestionably
	Quite irrefutably
	End
	– but who cares, –
	In tears!

Sophie enters with her costume which she hands to Amy

Sophie (*briefly*) The zip's a bit dodgy. And it's terribly scratchy round the neck. Can you do anything about it?
Laura (*hastily*) I'll have a look at it?
Amy (*frostily*) Anything else?
Sophie (*sweetly*) I don't think so – thank you.
Amy Where's Nick? I'm still waiting for his costume.
Sophie I have no idea. (*She crosses down to the fountain*)

Nick enters with his costume which he casually throws to Amy

Amy begins to fold it

Amy I suppose it's too much to ask you to turn the sleeves the right side out!

Nick grins

Tom enters

Tom Any chance of a lift Mike?

Amy flings Nick's costume into the skip

Amy (*brusquely*) Bring that!

Amy stalks off with Laura

Michael (*to Tom*) Yeah, you can squeeze in the back. Give us a hand with this.

Michael and Tom pick up the skip and exit

Sophie and Nick are left alone

Sophie I shall probably celebrate the last night by stuffing Amy into her portfolio and shoving her in the river.

26: Flora and Abigail

Katie enters quietly. She is startled to see them both

Katie I thought everybody had gone. (*She stands irresolutely by the fountain, as if she does not want to go*)
Nick You two coming for a drink?
Sophie OK.
Katie (*hesitating*) Do you want – is it all right if I —
Nick (*savagely*) Yes, or I wouldn't have asked you.
Katie That wasn't what I meant.
Nick Look, it's no big deal you having a go at me. I'm glad you did. It's better than you agreeing with me all the time.

Katie is about to say something else but changes her mind

Katie (*turning away* US) Sorry.

Nick and Sophie exchange exasperated glances

Nick (*spelling it out*) There-is-nothing-to-be-sorry-for!

There is a sudden cackle as a flock of geese flies overhead

Nick, Katie and Sophie watch quietly

Katie It's a shame isn't it? – All that's going to go.
Sophie (*scornfully*) You won't stop the geese! They fly over our flats now... A few executive houses aren't going to get in their way!
Katie Look, you two go on. I'll – I'll be along in a minute. I'd just like to stay here for a while.
Nick We're not leaving you here on your own. It's getting dark. It's probably not safe.
Katie (*running her hand down the pillar of the temple*) It looks marvellous now it's clean, doesn't it? It even feels better with all that – filth scrubbed off. Isn't it awful that it's going to be destroyed? After all these years.

Act II

Sophie Well, there's nothing we can do about it.
Katie Was this really a temple to Flora, Nick?
Nick No, I made that up. I don't know how old the real Flora was when it was built. She probably didn't even know the architect either – except to say good-morning. Makes a good story though.
Katie But she did disappear?
Nick Without trace.
Katie I wonder why.
Nick Your guess is as good as mine – that's the brilliant thing about history, you can make it all up.
Katie Isn't it terrible not knowing... I wonder what happened here.
Nick You came here looking for snails when you were six.
Sophie You don't even know that Flora ever came down this alleyway. She might have spent all her time indoors drinking chocolate and reading the latest horror novels.

Katie, Sophie and Nick stand still, a little sad

It is getting gradually darker

Katie (*quietly*) Why does everything have to be so sad? It wouldn't have hurt for things to go right for once. Why couldn't Mr Freshwater have said "No" to Greshams – "Certainly not. This must all be preserved and looked after and given to people who–"
Sophie Because he's a waste of air and Whittaker saw him first.

Nick moves away and sits by the fountain

Sophie Anyway, even if it was preserved and kept nice for everybody they'd soon ruin it. It'd be vandalized – full of funfairs and jumble sales and flashers. (*She moves DS and sits on the bench*)

Katie sits, leaning against the temple. They all seem unable to leave

The moon is beginning to appear mistily from behind the temple

Katie (*dreamily*) This is our place now isn't it? We belong here – I don't want to go away...

Flora enters, wearing a dress identical to the one Sophie wore earlier but it is worn, less vivid and not so glitteringly new. She is wearing a hooded cloak and carrying a reticule.

Abigail, her maid, follows her carrying a small carpet bag

Abigail Oh Miss Flora, please let me come with you. You can't go on your own. You'll be no more able to look after yourself than a baby.
Flora No, Abigail, you must stay here—
Abigail But where are you going? What are you going to do? Creeping out like a thief in the night. What shall I say if Captain Freshwater shouts at me? If he curses me and shouts at me and bullies me I know I won't be able to keep quiet —

Flora That's why I shall not tell you where I'm going. Then you cannot give me away.

Abigail Oh please —

Flora You may tell Captain Freshwater that I have gone – you do not know where. And I shall never – ever set foot anywhere I think *he* might be. I am dead – to him.

Abigail He would beat me.

Flora Yes, I am sure he would, so it's better if you know nothing.

Abigail Then I shall follow you.

Flora No, you must stay – and look after my sons. You are the only mother they will have now. You must care for them as I would. Don't – don't let them think ill of me. (*She turns away and takes a letter from her reticule*) Give this to Will, when he is old enough to understand —

Abigail Why are you leaving them – to him? He'll beat them as he beat you. How can you abandon them like that?

Flora Because that is the only way I can give them a life of their own. They will understand. If I stay their father will rob them of their inheritance. They will drag out a miserable existence – to which they are not fitted. But if I go – my going will make all well for them. This is the only way I can provide for my children...

Abigail Oh no, no, Miss Flora, you cannot. Don't!! I won't let you! (*She seizes Flora's skirts*)

Flora You silly child. Get up. I am **not** going to kill myself. But I shall be dead – to him. (*She turns away*)

Sophie rises and starts forward as if to speak to Flora

Flora obviously does not see Sophie

Katie (*quietly*) No Sophie, go back, she can't see you.

Sophie moves back again. Katie and Nick also remain in their positions

Flora When I know for certain that he is not here I shall come back. By the river... I shall wait and you can bring the boys so that I can see them.

Abigail What if he sends them away? You know he could do it. Shut this house up and send them away into the country – like a good loving father! And if he and that sister of his tell them that they have a wicked evil mother who ran away from them because she hated them, and they grow up to believe that, what will you do then?

Flora I shall hope that you will tell them the truth.

Abigail Please don't make me do this. Don't make me the guardian of your secrets. I'm not strong enough.

27: Flora's Farewell (Music XV)

Flora and Abigail begin in duet, with Abigail's lines intertwining with her mistress's melody

Flora Leaving	**Abigail** Dear Madam
Leaving	My lady
The sacred grove	My heart is too weak.

Act II

    Where my heart's joy
    My sweet boys, rove.
    Ah, now your mother
    Ah, now your mother
    Must seem, must seem to be dead.
    May guardian angels hover, hover
    Above each unprotected head.

    Weeping
    Weeping
    Such bitter tears.
    Forever goodbye
    My untroubled years.
    Into the shadows
    Into the shadows
    My sad shade, my sad shade must glide.
    May my undeserved sorrows
    Linger, linger forever by this waterside.

    My poor frail vessel
    Is bound to break.
    How will I bear it
    Seeing their sad tears.
    Their sad, sad tears.
    Seeing their sad, sad tears.

    The master,
    Your husband,
    Will beat me for sure.
    How can my spirit
    His passion endure?
    I'll do my duty
    As a good servant,
    A good servant should.
    As a good servant should.

Nick (*singing solo*)   Can a dream be solid flesh?
                                      What creation in a flash
                                      Makes a living
                                      Breathing being
                                      Of a dreamer's trash?

Sophie (*singing solo*)   So my eyes are liars too.
                                      Past is past, so let it go.
                                      Eyes deceive
                                      Go, just leave
                                      Soon.

Flora	**Abigail**	**Nick**
Leaving	Dear Madam	Can a dream be solid flesh?
Leaving	My Lady	What creation in a flesh
The sacred grove	My heart is too weak.	Makes a living
Where my heart's joy	My poor frail vessel	Breathing being
My sweet boys, rove.	Is bound to break.	Of a dreamer's trash?

Flora	**Abigail**	**Sophie**
Ah, now your mother	How will I bear it	So my eyes are liars too.
Ah, now your mother	Seeing their sad tears.	Past is past, so let it go.
Must seem, must seem to be dead.	Their sad, sad tears.	Eyes deceive
		Go, just leave
		Soon.

Flora and Abigail exit US

Katie (*singing solo*)   Living spirits dream here.
                                      "Never leave," they whisper.

The light on the centre stage fades and Sophie, Nick and Katie are left picked out by the moonlight. No-one moves. They are in exactly the same positions as they were when Flora and Abigail entered

Katie I don't want to go away... (*She rises and moves centre stage uncertainly looking round as if trying to remember something*)
Nick We can't stay here. Not now. It's too late.
Sophie (*getting up*) Oh come on, let's go. I hate it here. All these shadows.
Nick Afraid of the dark Sophie?
Sophie No, I just like to see where I'm going.
Joanna (*distantly calling; off stage*) Sophie! Nick! Katie! Where are you?
Sophie Coming.

Sophie exits quickly

Katie remains quite still

Nick Come on Katie, there's nothing here.

Nick takes Katie's hand and they exit

Black-out

28: The Card Game

There is a burst of noise and chattering

The Lights come up. It is a blazing and brilliant day

Laura, Amy, William, Michael, Tom, Jack and Chris enter with costumes, lights, cables and props etc. They begin to put up the lights, set out the props etc. Michael and Jack are wearing eighteenth century breeches and shirts. Laura and Amy carry bunches of flowers which they put in the urns

Jack, Tom and William put garlands on the statue by the fountain with shimmering streams of glittering silver paper and crystal beads, trailing down into the pool, turning it into a beautiful – artificial – working fountain

Amy brings across some waterlilies and drops them into the pool

Chris and Michael busy themselves with the lights

Louise and Emma enter and begin to set up a little card table with several flasks of 'red wine', glasses, packs of cards and biscuits on a silver tray

Joanna and Sue bring in a velvet screen and set it up behind the card table. Sue is carrying her props list

Louise, Emma, Joanna and Sue exit and return with four little chairs and set them round the table

Sue checks the props from her list

Sue Nobody is to touch the wine and biscuits. I've counted the biscuits and if

Act II

any go missing you can pay for them. (*Seeing the glasses*) Oh no! Can you not use real glasses till the Dress —
Jack Is it real wine?
Sue Ribena. But I know how much there is.
Laura Mike you'd better get the rest of your costume on or Charlotte'll kill you.
Michael She'll kill me anyway. I wish I didn't have to do this. I'm not an actor.
Louise No, we've noticed. But you are, I believe, male and the scene requires four fellas.
Laura And not even Nick at his most optimistic would let Chris loose on the stage.
Joanna (*drily*) What makes you think Michael is going to get onto the stage. I'll bet you ten to one he wanders into the river.
Amy Yes, you'd think that as Nick was writing to order he would have avoided the need to put all our incompetents on the stage in one scene.
Michael Thank you for your confidence in me. That makes it all worthwhile.
Louise Well, I think you're great, Mike. You'd be wonderful as the tree in the last act.

Danny and David enter, dressed as eighteenth century gentlemen

The girls collapse into giggles

Danny I *do* look as much of a prat as I feel then!
Louise Much more.
David Are you sure you're serious about this?
Danny Thought so. (*Gesturing to Michael*) Why isn't he wearing his nice costume then?
Amy I have slaved over these costumes. If you're going to be nasty about them I shall go home and take my safety pins with me. Are you going to wear those trainers?
Danny Well no, obviously not, but I can't walk in those poncy high heels you got me.
Laura You'll have to on the night. You'd better get used to them. Come on, Michael. Put these on... No, not just the jacket! Waistcoat as well. Charlotte's in a foul mood and if you're not ready to go she'll spit bone marrow.
Sue Do you want the glasses knocked over at the start of the scene – and the wine spilled?
Danny Just one. I'll knock the rest over in my passion.
Sue This all right? (*She arranges the glasses on the table*)
Danny Couldn't we have a white cloth then you could spill some wine artistically on it – to look like blood?
Sue *Four* white cloths. Six with the D.R.s. Or do you intend to wash them for me after each show?
Danny Just a thought.

Sue And you'll be using rehearsal props for now.
Danny How am I supposed to act with a plastic cup instead of a foaming beaker? They bounce!
Sue And glasses break. We can't afford any more.
Laura If you can act in trainers you can act a wine glass.

Nick, Sophie, Mark and Charlotte enter

Mark and Sophie are in full eighteenth century dress

Sophie stands in the temple

Nick settles down on the grass with a note book

Charlotte (*clapping her hands*) Right, break's over. Shut up everybody... I said shut up! We'll take it from where we left off. Positions please for the drinking scene.

Danny, Mark, David and Michael sit at the card table and begin to play cards. A long thoughtful pause as they look at their cards. They place their cards down on the table in turn, slowly and deliberately, except for Danny

Danny (*banging a card down*) Snap!

Everybody giggles, except Charlotte

Charlotte Danny! It's not funny! We open the day after tomorrow. Is that what you're going to do? And where are the glasses?
Sue Sorry Charlotte they'll be here for the Dress.
Charlotte They should be here now.
Sue I know. But they're not. And they will be.
Charlotte Let's hope so. OK Chris?
Chris (*off stage*) Yeah!
Charlotte OK. You needn't do the whole scene. Take it from "Do you dare accuse me of cheating?"
Danny OK. On your feet, Mark.

Danny seizes Mark by the lapels and shakes him

Danny Do you dare accuse me – *me* – of cheating?
Mark No, damme, but you win too often and too easily. And pay up too slowly when you lose.
Danny You dare say that to me. By God! I'll have you whipped and thrown into the river. And tell the world why I did it!
Mark Take your hands off me sir. I doubt that that would be wise. Do you think anyone would pay any attention to you, *Captain* Freshwater? Gambling away the money your wife brought to you—
Danny Why you! You!

Mark and Danny begin to struggle

David leaps up and separates them

Michael Stop! Are you both mad?

Danny and Mark glare at each other

David stares owlishly at them

David He's right, Harry, better leave him alone. Don't like the fella – but he's a lord. Can't throw a lord in the river. You're not even a baronet. Nobody'll come here if it gets about that you throw lords into the river. Throw me into the river. Nobody cares...I'm not even a Captain. Just a plain mister. No.. Where's my glass?

Michael He's right, Harry. Sit down. Finish the game.

Danny (*stiffly*) I beg your pardon, my Lord. I was angry. I did not think it was a nobleman's way to accuse a gentleman of cheating.

Mark Thank you sir. I take your apology and beg to inform you that you are mistaken. *I* did not say you were a cheat. That was an inf-inference you drew—

David This bottle's empty.

Michael And this one. Let us have more of your excellent wine. We are here to drink and play. Not to quarrel.

29: Drinking Song (Music XVI)

Danny	Sir, do not push me, You may go too far!
Mark	Sir, you're a scoundrel A brute and a bore!
Danny	Sir, you've insulted me, What should I think?
Michael	Sir, pick up your bumper And drown yourself in drink.
All	Fill up the beaker with foaming Falernian Bring the bright bubbles of brisk Beaujolais. Drink if you're English, or Welsh or Hibernian We'll drink till we're staggering drunk today.
Danny	Sir, I'm a terror With rapier and sword.
Mark	Sir, I've been told You're a pimp and a bawd.
Danny	Sir, with such language I can scarcely but choose...
David	Sir, top up the tumbler And soak up the booze.

All	Fill up the beaker with foaming Falernian Bring the bright bubbles of brisk Beaujolais. Drink if you're English, or Welsh or Hibernian We'll drink till we're staggering drunk today.
Danny	Sir, my enemies Are enemies for life.
Mark	Sir, you're a halfwit, And so is your wife.
Danny	Sir, you're a maniac!
Mark	Sir, you're a swine!
Michael	Sir, crack this bottle And sozzle in wine.
All	Fill up the beaker with foaming Falernian Bring the bright bubbles of brisk Beaujolais. Drink if you're English, or Welsh or Hibernian We'll drink till we're staggering drunk today!

Charlotte Go on. That's fine Chris!
Danny Wench!

Abby enters, dresses as Abigail

Danny More wine wench!
Abby Sir, may I speak with you?
David These bottles are empty. And I am hungry!
Abby Sir!
Danny Bring more food and wine for my friends and be quick!
Abby Sir, I must speak with you. Will and Jack—
Danny Who? Watch your disrespectful tongue, girl!
Abby — Master Will and Master Jack have not come back yet sir, from their ride. They went with you, sir, and you have been back for more than an hour. We have been watching and looking out for them but there is no sign of them. It is dark, sir, you have dined and – oh sir! – should the grooms be sent to look for them? Please sir...
Danny Stop snivelling. And bring me some wine. The boys galloped off on their own. Yes, and I let them. They've got some spirit those lads of mine. They don't need you mollycoddling them. My sons are going to grow up to be men. Not namby-pamby, poetry-spouting weaklings, tied to some woman's apron strings. Fetch me some food and some wine.

Danny grabs Abby by the arm and takes her DS

I know why you creep round those boys and I'll not have it, do you hear? Now get out. If my sons choose to take off on their own account they don't need your permission. When they get back, you are to keep away from them. I'm not having 'em made soft by you on *her* orders. If I hear you have so much as spoken to them I'll have you thrown out, bag and baggage and you can follow her!

Abby exits followed by Jack

Danny crosses to the table and sits frowning

David Wouldn't matter if you threw her in the river. (*He roars with laughter at the idea*)

David, Mark, Michael and Danny freeze

The Lights fade on them and a pool of light comes up by the fountain

30: Hilary Returns

Charlotte That's lovely, Chris, but you can take the fade even slower. Sophie, start coming in as they freeze so that the light finds you. OK Chris, let's just have that crossfade again. Stand by Sophie, Jack. Thank you, Danny. Just the cross.

Jack reappears by the temple

Danny moves back to the table and sits down

David (*with no expression*) Wouldn't matter if you threw her in the river, Har Har Har.

The Lights fade as before. Danny, Mark, Michael and David freeze

The Lights come up on Sophie, muffled in her cloak

Sophie (*peering out into the darkness*) Abigail, is that you?

Black-out

Charlotte That's not quite what I meant Chris...
Chris It's not what I meant either Charlotte. Damn and blast this bloody — (*He becomes incoherent*)

There is laughter and noise in the dark

David Be all right if you threw him in the river.

There are gales of mirth

Chris All right Dave, if you're so bloody clever you come and do the sodding lights.
Charlotte Thank you, Chris. It's a beautiful black-out but could we possibly have some light. Somewhere. Please?

Chris stalks off

After a moment, a very prosaic work light comes up

Charlotte Thank you. What's the problem and how long will it take to put it right?

Chris enters

Chris I don't know. About three hours I should think.
Charlotte You've got twenty minutes.
Chris What!? Do me a favour! Look I'm sorry.
Charlotte So am I. OK everybody. Relax.
Chris Mike! Don't just sit there. Come and do something.

Michael gets up with a rueful grin and exits with Chris

Danny Don't get your frock dirty!

Charlotte goes US abruptly and stares up at the lights, then broods up and down

Abby, William and Jack cross to sit with Sophie by the fountain

Nick goes over to Sophie

Katie enters with a plastic cup of coffee which she takes to Charlotte, then she joins Nick and Sophie

Hilary enters DS and stands watching quietly

No-one sees her for a moment

Sophie (*taking Nick's notebook away from him*) No, no more changes. I've learned it and that's what I'm going to say. If you don't like it you can do the other thing.
Nick The mood Charlotte's in you'll do as you're told.
Sophie The mood Charlotte's in she'll shove your new lines where they will cause you most discomfort. (*Very sweetly*) How are you getting on, Chris?

Chris emerges onto the stage

Chris Look, just get off my back will you? I've got enough problems without you trying to be clever.
Michael (*calling from off stage*) Chris, Don't wander off. We'll never get this done.
Chris ALL RIGHT!!!

Chris exits

Sophie giggles and stretches and looks round. She nudges Katie

Sophie Well, Well, Well. (*Loudly*) Hallo, Mrs Osbourne. What a surprise.

There is silence

Everyone looks at Hilary

Chris and Michael enter

Hilary crosses with assumed asurance

Act II

Charlotte (*amused; looking her up and down*) Did you have a nice holiday?
Hilary Very nice. Thank you. (*Pause*) Well – no need to ask you how things are going. Amazing differences here since I saw you last.
Charlotte Oh there's nothing like a good lost cause to get the adrenalin flowing. We've worked so hard you might almost have thought it was worth our while!
Sophie (*sweetly*) We get our reward the day after tomorrow. Greshams have put in block bookings for every performance. Isn't that nice of them? We're nearly sold out. So if you haven't got a ticket yet – I don't know if you'll get in.
Hilary (*biting her lip*) I see. Look I'm awfully sorry. This was a mistake. You don't want me around. I can understand that – shall I just disappear?
Nick You were in at the beginning you might as well be in at the death.
Katie I don't suppose you've – nothing's come up has it? Have you heard anything – had any ideas?
Hilary Nary a one I'm afraid. I've never been so scuppered. Mr Freshwater won't reconsider. He wants to play fair and Greshams got him first. They're sorting out the fine print. You haven't had any bright ideas?

There is a pause

Charlotte That was supposed to be your department.
Nick No, we've just been feeling pretty choked. We don't like being rail-roaded into something and then abandoned. We feel a bit bloody stupid the way we've been hijacked to make an advert for Greshams.
Mark I just wish we could get it clear who we're supposed to be doing this show for... Next week a charity matinée for knackered guide dogs.
Charlotte It hasn't been too easy doing the show, feeling the way we do. And that's the understatement of the year.
Katie As far as the play's concerned we've been working so hard it's been just like any other play. But-it's the place. It was just a filthy stinking wasteland when we first came here but – we all feel the same – it isn't me being moonstruck – we belong here now. It matters. There's something here that—
Hilary Yes, I know. (*Slight pause*) I had an awful holiday actually. I just kept thinking about here. Simon's still in Crete. Don't suppose he'll want to know me when he gets back either. But I had to come back and see how you were getting on.

31: Failures (Music XVII)

The Chorus sing in unison, stamping their feet, clapping their hands, banging tables and chairs or any other useful object, as indicated in score

Chorus We're not getting on.
We're getting angry.
We don't like being used
By Whittaker and his mob.
We feel like going home,
We're tired and hungry,

And our play's been hi-jacked
As part of a P.R. job.

Hilary and Charlotte duet, with Charlotte's acid comments interweaving with Hilary's lyrical line

Hilary Why did I walk away?   **Charlotte** Some people.
I don't understand. Who needs 'em?
That's not my usual way. No action
When I get a job in hand All talk, all talk.
That job gets done. Good causes.
But this one... She leads 'em.
Why did I turn my back and go? First setback.
I don't know. Takes a walk.

What is it draws me back? Ignore her
Something about the place She's useless
Sets my mind on a one way track Self pity
A temple, a grove, a face... Moaning on,
    moaning on.
There was no holiday Coming here.
From your play Making speeches
As though you'd set up your Sign of trouble
  stage in my brain
I can't explain Oh, she's gone!

I've always tried to help Failures,
To do the best I can. Let you down.
One must never give up hope That'll teach us,
There's so much to be done. Hard way to learn,
    hard way to learn.
When such passionate belief Never rely on
Comes to grief People's good will.
How can the energy and Shoulder to cry on
  hope return?
I'll have to learn. Won't pay the bill.

Chorus We're not getting on,
We're getting angry!

As the song ends the Lights come up

32: Flora's Tragedy

Chris Am I a genius or am I a genius?

The group disperses with ironic applause

  Chris exits. Sophie runs off stage. Jack exits

Hilary Well, I'd better be going, I suppose.

Katie No, don't go. Unless you want to – we'll be starting the Dress Rehearsal soon... It wasn't your fault.
Hilary No, it wasn't but that doesn't stop me feeling guilty. I ran away...I seem to be running off in all directions don't I?... I've never done that before....

There is a pause

Katie Nick? Charlotte?
Nick Stay as far as I'm concerned.

Charlotte looks at Hilary with an odd kind of pitying contempt.

Charlotte (*quietly*) You could say you've taught us a valuable lesson.
Hilary Oh?
Charlotte Work it out.
Hilary (*wincing*) Yes, you obviously didn't need me. (*Changing the subject*) I'm dying to see what you've done.
Charlotte Right, can we get on? Clear the stage please. We OK now Chris?
Chris (*off*) OK.
Charlotte Positions please, gamblers.

David, Michael, Mark and Danny take their places wearily and the Lights repeat their earlier cue

Charlotte Sophie? (*She looks round*) Sophie! Where's she disappeared to? I wish people wouldn't slope off when they're needed! (*She darts an ironic glance at Hilary*) Sophie! Flora on stage please!

Some of the others join in the call for Sophie

Sophie rushes on with a sandwich in her hand

Sophie Sorree! (*She puts the sandwich on the card table*) Don't touch that! (*She takes up her position in the pool of light by the fountain*)
Charlotte Quiet please... Shut up! Cue Sophie.
Sophie Abigail – is that you?

Jack enters in riding gear, muddy and dishevelled

Jack (*in a quiet strained voice*) Mama you must come quickly. Will is... Satan threw him – And I think his neck is broken. His head is twisted and – he he doesn't move.

Sophie stands quite still

Jack Mama – he was riding Satan.
Sophie What?
Jack Papa laughed at him and said he was a baby, riding his girl's pony – and Will – Will said he wasn't afraid and he could ride Satan. And Papa laughed and said he was a brave fellow and he told me to keep out of sight – and Will rode away and I couldn't keep up with him and... and... I found him... Satan had gone.
Sophie Where is he?
Jack The other side of the park. By the bridge. (*He breaks down*)

Abby enters the pool of light from US

Abby (*distressed*) Oh, my Lady —
Sophie (*comforting Jack*) Sssssh! You have been very brave. But you must be braver yet. Go to your Papa and tell him —
Jack Oh Mama, won't you come with me? He will be angry with me.
Sophie No, I cannot, Jack. You must go. If – if Will is dead – you must be the master. You must not tell your father that you have seen me or everything will be lost. Go now, I shall go – to find Will – to see him one last time. I shall not be there when you come to find him. But I will be here to see you. Sometime... Go quickly!

Jack moves away centre stage

Danny leaves the table and moves DS, so that he is standing on the opposite side of the stage from Sophie

Flora, hooded like Sophie, enters US and stands in the temple

33: Elegy (Music XVIII)

Sophie
(*singing solo*)
Ah, gods,
My heart is breaking;
No earthquake, tempest shaking
The world to pieces can match my grief,
A mother's anguish. There's no relief
From this eternity of pain.
My son is gone
Where none can follow.
He will never return.
Mine is the sorrow.

Danny
(*singing solo*)
Ah, gods,
The world is breaking.
No hint of tears, no shaking
Of the lip. A man must hide his grief,
Show a father's courage. His relief
Is to deny the pain.
My boy is gone.
May I soon follow.
Why haste to return
To this vale of sorrow?

Jack's following music may be sung by Abby, embracing Jack as she sings, if this is more convenient. In that case the word "brother" should be changed to "darling"

Jack
(*singing solo*)
Will, my poor brother,
Where have you gone?
Into the darkness,

Act II

> Under a stone.
> What ghastly nightmare
> Sleeps with you there?
> Death is a terror
> That lurks everywhere.

Flora, unseen by Sophie, Danny and Jack, sings solo

Flora
> No call for anguish,
> No time for pain,
> The face of sorrow
> Is blank and plain.
> The gift of your life, my darling boy,
> Was a short, but everlasting joy.
> Farewell, sweet Will, child of my youth.
> Cover him softly, gentle earth.

All four sing in quartet, unaccompanied

Sophie
> My son is gone
> Where none can follow.
> He will never return.
> Mine is the sorrow.

Danny
> My boy is gone.
> May I soon follow.
> Why haste to return
> To this vale of sorrow?

Jack
> What ghastly nightmare
> Sleeps with you there?
> Death is a terror
> That lurks everywhere.

Flora
> Farewell, sweet Will, child of my youth.
> Cover him softly, gentle earth.

When the song ends Danny, Jack and Sophie relax

Flora remains in the temple

Charlotte Thank you. Three quarters of an hour. Everybody back at half past sharp. (*She crosses up to the group by the table*)

Charlotte, David, Michael, Mark and Danny exit, talking

Tom, William, Amy, Laura, Louise, Emma, Sue and Abby exit severally

Sophie takes off her cloak and drops it on the bench. She retrieves her sandwich and sits eating it

Hilary, Nick and Katie move centre stage

Jack stays by the fountain

34: The Spirit Of The Place

Sophie Not a dry eye in the house.
Hilary Very good. Is that you or history, Nick?
Nick Bit of both. Flora Freshwater's eldest son died in a riding accident. The estate was held in trust for her sons and administered on their behalf in the event of her death. Her husband never got his hands on her house or her money and died flat broke. Flora disappeared without trace. The rest is me. Who's to say it didn't happen like that?
Sophie Except they say she drowned.
Nick Didn't find a body though, did they? I like to think of her flitting mysteriously through the trees keeping an eye on her beloved sons and her beloved house... Anyway – I like to see Sophie pretending to have feelings.
Hilary Sounds more like Katie!

There is a pause

Sophie Nine out of ten for going to Crete; Ten out of ten for tact.
Hilary Was she buried?
Sophie Who? Flora?
Nick I don't know. I don't think so. If she *was* a suicide they wouldn't have buried her in consecrated ground.
Hilary And her second son took over the estate?
Jack That's me. In the next episode.
Nick Suppose so.
Sophie We stopped at that point. Took us long enough to find out as much as we did. Specially trying to track down Flora.
Jack That old lady's called Flora.

Flora exits silently

Sophie I'm not surprised. There were millions of them in the eighteenth century. And Sophies.
Katie What old lady?
Jack You know. She walks along the towpath very early in the mornings. Haven't you seen her?
Katie No.
Sophie You must have. She's always dressed in grey. Never speaks to anybody. Lives in that narrow house by the Church. She sits in the graveyard most afternoons. Haunts the place — (*She stops as if trying to remember something*)
Nick Oh yes, I've seen her.
Katie Flora.

They all stand quite still for a long moment

Katie shivers

Hilary What's the matter?
Katie Nothing. A goose walked over my grave.
Sophie I was going to say something... No, it's gone.
Hilary I wonder where this Mr Freshwater fits in.

Act II

Nick In Whittaker's pocket that's where. Come on let's go and get some food.

Nick, Sophie and Jack exit, chatting

Katie stays looking around

Hilary Aren't you coming, Katie?
Katie There must be something wrong with me. I always like places better when everybody else has gone... You shouldn't like places better than people should you? I can't bear the thought of this place... being killed.
Hilary You mustn't think like that – It's unhealthy... I feel very bad about my unheroic part in all this. I don't know what possessed me... stopped me seeing things clearly. I'm very sorry I let you down.
Katie It doesn't matter. (*Quickly*) Please don't apologize to me. I don't need it. I haven't got an opinion about you – one way or the other.
Hilary (*taken aback*) Oh, I – see.
Katie I didn't mean to be rude. It's just that it doesn't matter what any of us do, does it? And that's a pity. They'd still be ripping this place up if we'd *all* gone to Crete. You go on. I'll catch you up.
Hilary I'll wait for you by the gate —
Katie Why will nobody ever let me – I just want to be here – by myself for two minutes. And there's always a crowd!
Hilary Then I won't wait by the gate.

Hilary exits quickly

Katie (*closing her eyes*) Oh please, let it be all right!.

Faint music is heard very softly off stage, and then, as though from a great distance, Flora's voice, singing Nick's counter melody to "Leaving"

35: Second Reprise of Leaving (Music XIX)

Flora (*singing off stage*)
>Leaving,
>Breaking my heart.

Katie listens, as though hearing music in the air, then crosses to the bench and picks up Sophie's cloak and puts it on, wrapping it around her. She closes her eyes in an agony of intensity, and stands listening

>Leaving,
>Living apart now,
>Crying,
>Hiding my tears,
>Trying,
>To stifle my fears that,

Flora enters singing, and Katie sees her (N.B. See Production note on p. vii)

>Leaving
>Is breaking my heart,
>Leaving
>You alone.

As Flora comes to the centre of the stage repeating Nick's countermelody, Katie sings the melody, almost at though trying to persuade her

Flora does not see Katie

Flora	Leaving.	**Katie**	Leaving,
	Breaking my heart,		Drifting apart.
	Leaving,		Leaving,
	Living apart now,		What if your heart says
	Crying,		Stay here,
	Hiding my tears,		Give it a chance,
	Trying		Don't go,
	To stifle my fears that		Even a trance like
	Leaving		Dreaming
	Is breaking my heart,		's an honester way
	Leaving		Than going
	You alone.		Too soon.

Flora exits

Katie moves quickly to where she was, looking for her

Katie slowly exits as:

The music fades away

36: George's Gift

The Lights come up to full on the empty stage

David mooches on disconsolately. He sits down and takes out a newspaper staring at it moodily

Michael and Tom enter carrying fairy lights and a ladder

Michael You're early.
David I know. It was a mistake. I thought we were starting at seven. God, it's hot. I'm going to melt in that jacket. Have you seen this?
Michael What?
David Local Paper. All over the middle pages. Artist's impression of the Freshwater Grove – huh! – town houses. We're sitting on somebody's patio by the looks of things.

Michael crosses and looks at the newspaper

Michael Mmm. Pity.
David Pretty naff aren't they? Not even 'proposed' any more you notice. "The delightful Neo-Georgian houses that Gresham Developments *will* be building..." We're in the small print on the page with the jumble sales!
Michael Oh well, can't be helped, I suppose.
Tom Look, am I doing these lights on my own? (*He begins to string up the fairy lights*)

Act II

George Freshwater comes in carrying a large bulging carrier bag

George Ah, nobody here yet then?
David (*looking round*) Apparently not. Just us.
George Oh how terribly rude of me! I meant the – erm – well, whoever's in charge – of your play, I mean.

David clicks his heels and does a Hitler salute

David You mean Charlotte.
George Do I?
David She won't be long. We're early. We've got a Dress Rehearsal.
George The big night is tomorrow, yes?
David Yup. You coming?
George Oh yes, Mr Whittaker is bringing a party.
David That's all we need...
George Ah, yes... Mmm... (*trying again*) Tell me, where do you get all the -er- costumes and scenery and so on, from?
David Hire some of it. Make most of it. Cadge the rest.
George I see. Is that very difficult?
David Dunno really. I don't have anything to do with the technical side. I just do the acting —
Michael That's his story and he's sticking to it.

Nick, Amy and Charlotte enter. They glance briefly at George with some surprise

Charlotte crosses to Michael and begins to supervise the positions of the fairy lights

Nick picks up David's newspaper and stares at it gloomily

Amy takes out a length of velvet ribbon from her bag and begins to sew a little 'Cameo' onto it

George Er, excuse me. Could I have a word with you?
Amy Me?
George Are you Charlotte?
Charlotte No, that's me.
George You're the producer?
Charlotte Yes.
George How do you do. Well. I really wanted to – look, I'm very sorry indeed about all this.
Nick Why apologize to us? It's your land. You can sell it to who you like. I hope you got a good price for it!
George No, that's not what I meant. What I really wanted to say was I'm sorry I've put you in such a difficult position by turning up. I can see it makes doing your play very difficult. Pretty embarrassing and all that. I don't like ill-feeling – and well, I wondered ... I don't know anything about plays, you know, but... what's that you're doing?
Amy This? I'm making a choker for Joanna to wear.

George Where did you get the cameo?
Amy Made it.
George May I? (*He inspects the cameo*) Well, well, that's awfully good!

Amy, Nick, Charlotte, David, Tom and Michael are amused

Amy (*gravely hiding her giggles*) Just a knack and a bit of plaster of Paris.
George Well now, that's the thing. Now, I don't know if it's any use to you but – I've rooted round at home and got together a few family bits and pieces. And there's some old jewellery there. There's not much and there's nothing valuable – but I wondered if they'd be any use to you – for your play. A little peace offering... Of course it may be no use at all.
Amy (*touched*) Oh, that's really kind of you!

George hands the carrier bag to Charlotte

Charlotte (*briefly*) Thanks. You'd better go through it Amy. (*She turns away*)

There is a very faint rumble of thunder in the distance

Was that thunder?
David I hope so.

Amy takes the bag and begins to look through it. She pulls out letters, photographs, diaries, a leather-bound book, and finally, a small box, which she opens

Amy (*holding up a jet necklace and a brooch*) Oh, this is brilliant!
George It's mourning jewellery. When you had a bereavement, you always decked yourself out in jet.
Amy It's beautiful. Sophie can wear that.
George It *is* Victorian.
Amy Never mind.

Nick crosses over, picks up a letter and glances briefly at it

Nick (*handing the newspaper to George*) You'd better add this to your collection.
George That won't be necessary. I think they're very attractive houses.
David Don't exactly blend with the houses round there though do they. *They're* mostly pokey little two-up-two-downers. Mind you, most of them have been gentrified.
George Yes, my family apparently built those as well! Edmund, my great-great grandfather – that was his wife's jewellery.
Tom Did you really not know anything about this place, till Whittaker found you?
George No, I'm not really interested in the past per se. Enough trouble keeping up with the present! Specially in farming nowadays. I knew the family had been very wealthy indeed, and owned property in London, but I didn't take much notice. Most families have some such legends about how rich they used to be.
Nick True in your case though.

George Well, in a way. The reason I'm in Lincolnshire is that my great-grandfather had to sell up and move out to the country, because he was so broke. There was a vast amount of money, but great-great-grandpa blew the lot. Or not, depending on your point of view! He sold off the park land, and built all the houses at his own expense. He was a wild-eyed do-gooder. Spent every last penny on the poor. He thought if you gave the working-classes decent houses, they'd turn into decent people! So all my great-grandpa got was the house itself, which he eventually had to sell off to make ends meet. Sad little tale, isn't it?

Nick Depends on where you're standing.

Amy (*taking an exquisite lace collar and putting it round her neck*) Look at this lace, it's so fine! We daren't use that. I'd love to though. It's nice, isn't it – the real thing?

The dawn music can be heard faintly

There is a strange pause as even Amy is affected by the atmosphere

George Well, I hope they're some use to you, those things. I've found it fascinating – being handed my family history on a plate. I'd never have gone into it myself – but I am getting quite interested. There are all sorts of odd little corners. For instance, Edmund wouldn't let the architect do anything with this bit. He was full of all sorts of potty William Morris-y ideas about enriching people's lives spiritually. Suppose it was the time he lived in – but – he wanted the people here to have music and poetry in their lives. Ordinary labourers, mark you! There's a pile of letters about it there. He sounds a bit of a frost actually – terribly dull read. But he had this bee in his bonnet, so this bit was set aside for the good of their souls, and the detriment of his purse! That's where all the money went, uneconomic rents, and entertainments for the plebs. Rich man's whim. They can afford 'em. It's called Flora's Walk.

Nick What?

George This alley-way – park. It's called Flora's Walk.

Nick Is it, begad!

Tom Flora's Walk.

There is a peal of thunder, and the sound of sudden heavy rain

Charlotte That is all we need!

Zoë rushes in with an umbrella

Zoë Oh there you are, Mr Freshwater! Mr Whittaker was wondering where you'd got to. Would you like to come this way, I've got the car?

George Oh, very well... Goodbye then – till tomorrow night.

George and Zoë exit

David Come on, let's shelter in your van Mike.

Charlotte Don't leave those lights!

Michael No, I know, give me a hand.

David, Tom and Michael take down the fairy lights

Amy collects up the jewellery and lace etc., and puts it in her bag
Nick stuffs the letters, diaries etc. back into the carrier bag
They all prepare to rush away

Charlotte Come on Nick, you'll get soaked!
Nick No, you go. I'll shelter in the temple. It's only a shower.

Charlotte, David, Michael, Tom and Amy exit with the fairy lights Amy's bag and the ladder

37: Flora's Walk (Music XX)

Nick What does it matter, standing in the rain?
In the corners of my brain
Something strange is happening.
A thought I can't yet understand,
A tune I can't quite hear:
Something gentle touching my hand...
Flora, somehow, somewhere.

"Where Flora walks..."
But Flora walked here.
How did I know that?
What does it mean?
Didn't I create her,
Make her re-appear?
But I can't deny
What my eyes have seen.

I saw her leaving.
Was I in a trance?
Choosing the shadows
Something like death.
Destroying her life
For her sons' inheritance.
Why did she show me
That moment of truth?

And why did Edmund,
Who sold the rest,
Built workmen's houses
On his father's park
Preserve this temple
And forever blessed
This grove with her name:
Flora's Walk?

Who are her children?
Why did she appear?
Who will inherit

These temples, this grass?
Why does her sad shade
Still walk here?
We are her children.
It belongs to us.

38: After the Storm

Nick exits, carrying the bag full of letters

The thunder and lightning die away

The moon is coming up

Sophie enters. She is extremely fed up. She crosses to the platform and runs her hand along it. It is 'wet'. She looks round

Sophie Yergh! Wonderful!

Nick enters

Sophie They all still in the pub?
Nick Yeah.
Sophie So we don't start till after closing time! Marvellous! I've heard of some crazy ideas, but starting a D.R. at half past eleven at night in a mud bath is the best yet! Everywhere's still soaking wet.
Nick No, we're not doing anything else tonight. Even Charlotte's seen sense. The thought of Chris, the lights, a thunderstorm and wet grass finally got through to her. We'll just have to have the one Dress tomorrow morning.
Sophie We're supposed to get this shambles on with one Dress?
Nick You've really enjoyed yourself on this show haven't you.
Sophie What's that supposed to mean?
Nick Well you haven't exactly thrown yourself into it heart and soul, have you?
Sophie Oh, thanks a lot! I've been word perfect with all your lines – and all your re-writes – since day one – well nearly. I've come rushing here from work, absolutely exhausted, and rehearsed my socks off, with everybody getting at me. You think I don't know that Amy and Laura can't stand me? What more do you want – blood?
Nick All right, all right, forget it. Sorry.
Sophie It's no better at home. Mum looks like it's her birthday and Christmas all in one if I say I'm going out. She can't wait to see the back of me. She loved it being all pallsy and just like sisters really, till Uncle bloody Trevor came along. Now all I've got is nuisance value. She's the one who'd really love it if I was rehearsing till four in the morning. I don't give damn about this place. I can't wait till it's all over.
Nick What are you going to do then?
Sophie Go away somewhere. Abroad. I don't know. I've got some money. Just go away for a while.

Nick Will you come back here?
Sophie (*shrugging*) I've grown out of all this. I used to love it, but it all seems so childish now.
Nick Thanks a lot.
Sophie Oh, don't you start being all hurt. I don't mean you.
Nick It may well be a shambles tomorrow. And it may not be up to much. But I did write this play for you.
Sophie (*uncertainly; looking at him*) No you didn't.
Nick I thought I did.
Sophie Well, you've got nothing to worry about. It's quite good. Everybody'll love it. Doesn't matter what I think. You don't really like me anyway. Not really.
Nick Now you're getting paranoid.
Sophie No I'm not. People keep getting at me. Nobody really likes me when they get to know me.
Nick (*disgusted*) Oh Sophie, don't be so self-indulgent.

Katie enters

Sophie Enter Tinkerbell. Do you think if I clap my hands she'll drop down dead?
Katie Sorry, am I interrupting?
Sophie No, you're not.
Katie Hilary's in the pub, Nick. You wanted to talk to her. Charlotte says to tell you rehearsal's an hour earlier tomorrow.
Sophie I may or may not be there.
Nick You'd better be there. I may or may not have some interesting news.
Sophie Oh goody goody.
Katie What's the matter, Sophie?
Nick Oh, she's in a lovely mood. Ignore her.
Katie So's everybody else. It's terrible in the pub. It's a wonder Ted hasn't thrown us all out.
Sophie Well, never mind, Katie. There's a little bit of good news coming your way. I'm leaving. So you can trail round after Nick to your heart's content, without falling over me all the time.

There is a momentary pause, then Katie slaps Sophie's face very hard

There is a pause

Katie (*quietly*) I'm sorry, I shouldn't have done that. That was acting like you. If you're feeling miserable there's no need to lash out at everybody else. No, not everybody else – me. It doesn't hurt you if I – if I trail round after Nick. And it might do you good if you didn't get exactly what you wanted for once. You've got everything. You haven't got the slightest idea how humiliating it is to – to be me.
Nick Oh my God. Couldn't you save the histrionics till tomorrow? I'm going down the pub. I've got things to do. You two can have a nice emotional work out, but could you leave me out of it please?

Nick exits

Act II

There is a pause

Sophie You'd better go after him.
Katie No.
Sophie He's not worth it.
Katie (*bitterly*) I'll probably leave it for about ten minutes.

Sophie shrugs and moves away DS and stands, lost in thought, her back to Katie

Katie I'm sorry I hit you.
Sophie I like provoking people. I thought Charlotte might have taken a swing at me by now, but not you.

Dawn music plays. Flora enters. She moves DS through the temple

The two figures in their identical dresses are on either side of Katie

Katie Are you really going away?
Sophie Yes.
Katie Why?
Sophie Because I've told everybody I'm going to. I'll just pack up and go as far as I can.
Flora And never come back.

Katie looks at Flora unsurprised

Sophie does not see Flora

Katie (*looking at Flora*) I don't think I could ever do that. I hate going to new places.
Sophie Well, when you've made a big enough mess in one place, you might as well just pack up and go. I shall take off my costume and make up, and disappear.
Flora Running. Running as fast as you can, away from yourself.
Sophie I'll look you all up one day. Tell you how I've got on.
Katie (*still looking at Flora*) I think you're very brave.
Sophie Oh, do me a favour, I'm only going on holiday, and then off to University, as a *slightly* mature student. I'm not walking to Katmandu.
Katie (*turning to Sophie*) You're walking out on everything else though aren't you?
Sophie Yup.
Flora Flora, you left this place in anguish, as an act of will. But part of you must always stay here — Flora.
Katie Flora. Flora's Walk.

39: The Real Flora (Music XXI)

Flora　　　　　　　The last time I was here,
(*singing solo*)　　　The last meeting,
　　　　　　　　　　There was mist on the water,
　　　　　　　　　　Summer was going.

	The last evening, The last goodbye, The price of leaving. The price of leaving. The last walk with my sons, Counting the cost, Understanding what I'd lost. Leaving, Going away, Leaving, For ever.
Sophie	Take off the costume, Put it away. I'm finished with playing After this play. What happened in the park Wearing a dead woman's dress, Walking Flora's walk Sharing her loneliness? You understand things here, I made the break. I'm going. Next week I'll disappear, Never quite knowing Who I'm deceiving, Which of us is leaving, Leaving.
Katie	Little girl on her knees Looking for snails in the park. What lingers in the trees, Why do I keep coming back? What am I obeying? Why am I staying? The past and the present are one, The going and the gone In an everlasting summer, Walking with Flora In the gathering dark: Always summer in the park.

Nick enters

The music continues under the following dialogue

Nick Come on you two. Don't hang around here. They're all waiting for you. *(Slightly puzzled)* Katie? Sophie?
Katie You came back...

Act II   75

Flora For Sophie. But she has gone...

Nick (*solo*)   Two women wear the same dress:
                         On of them lives in my head.
                         Of all places this is her place,
                         But she is centuries dead.

Flora   ⎫ (*singing*   The last days of summer
Katie   ⎬ *together*) Are almost here.
Sophie ⎭   Another season over,
                           Another year.

                         Nick The other girl I created too,
                         But she refused her part,
                         Left my created world to follow
                         The truth of her own heart.

Flora   Something is always leaving
Katie   Under the trees.
Sophie   A sigh like centuries passing
                         Across distant seas.

Nick   The third wears her own clothes
                         And she stands quietly between.
                         She is strong enough to chose
                         To stay where she's always been.

Flora   Something is always dying
Sophie   And coming to birth.
Katie   The mortal, joyous, grieving
                         Tenants of earth.

Flora, Sophie and Katie drift off slowly in opposite directions

Nick   The real Flora walked here
                         This place was her home.
                         My Flora is two girls in one,
                         A poet's dream.

                         Dreams tell me the deeper truth,
                         Poetry speaks what I feel:
                         That people who tread the common earth
                         Must be content with the real.

He looks round at the empty stage as the orchestra plays the Leaving theme

Nick slowly exits in the same direction Katie has taken

40: The Battle Won?

The Lights come up full and blazing. A brilliant summer's morning after the storm

Tom and Chris enter with the ladder and begin setting up the fairy lights

Gary mooches on, with his camera and a discontented expression. He glances briefly at Tom and Chris, then crosses and stares in disbelief at the fountain with all the glitter.

Gary Did you do that?
Tom *(looking round from his task)* What? Oh that, yeah.
Gary What's it supposed to be?
Tom A fountain.

Gary looks at him to make sure he is not being sent up. Then he looks at the fountain again, and shrugs

Gary Oh. *(He sits down dispiritedly and examines his camera)* You haven't seen Liz have you? Liz Mackie?
Tom
Chris } *(together)* No. Who's Liz Mackie?

Mrs Pagett and Mrs Weekly enter

Mrs Weekly All ready for the big night then are we?
Chris Nope.
Tom Haven't had our Dress Rehearsal yet. That storm last night —
Mrs Pagett Oh I know! Wasn't it terrible? So sudden. I thought about you lot.
Mrs Weekly I said to Ron, this'll put paid to their costumes —
Mrs Pagett Did you get wet?
Tom No, we were still in the pub.

Liz rushes in

Liz Oh there you are, Gary. I said I'd see you by the gates —
Gary Did you? Oh.
Liz Where's Mrs Osbourne?
Gary Who? You didn't say anything about the gates –
Liz Oh never mind! *(She looks round)* Well you've made a few changes round here... What exactly is going on?
Tom A Dress Rehearsal. We got rained off last night.
Mrs Weekly Then it's the show isn't it? *(To Liz)* You've got to have a Dress Rehearsal before the show...
Mrs Pagett Oh I can't wait! I've got my seat. Middle of the front row.
Liz Is that all? Your Mrs Osbourne was in a fantastic state about something —
Mrs Weekly She's not our Mrs Osbourne, dear.
Chris 'Scuse me! *(He carries the ladder across in front of Liz)*

Liz skips out of the way

Liz I shall be very cross if I've been dragged here for nothing.
Gary Shall we go then?
Liz No, hang on! We'd better wait till she gets here... And Gary, try not to cut all the heads off this time, eh?
Gary I don't like taking pictures of people. I'd rather do flower shows and funny vegetables. And bits of rubbish at low tide. I'm not ambitious...

Act II

Liz No, but I am. Ah there you are.

Hilary enters in a tearing hurry

Liz What's all this about then?
Hilary Just let's give it a minute. Till everybody gets here.

Michael, Joanna, Jack, William, Katie, Sophie, Amy, Laura, Louise, Emma, Sue, David, Mark, Danny, Nick, Abby and Charlotte enter with props, set dressings etc, with the characters from the play in their costumes

Nick Sorry I'm late. *(Excitedly to Hilary)* Well?
Hilary Yes! I think so!
Nick Great! Listen everybody! Something's cropped up.
Hilary Don't get too excited, but I think we may have something. It looks as though this piece of land, Flora's Walk, actually belongs to the community already! Not the Freshwater Estate. And – building on it is strictly forbidden!

The Company give huge cheers and begin to celebrate

Nick I've been here there and everywhere this morning trying to get things – but, Flora's great-great-grandson, Edmund, willed this place to everybody, for the pursuance of Music and Art, for ever! And as long as it's used for that purpose, no one can touch it.

There are more cheers

Hilary There's a long way to go yet, but at least the bulldozers can't move in.
Charlotte How did you get on to all this?
Hilary Ask Nick.
Nick It was when Mr Freshwater said this was called Flora's Walk —
Katie Flora's great-great-grandson!
Nick Yes.

There is an outburst of excited questions. Mr Whittaker enters, in a rage followed by Zoë Dean and Mr Freshwater

Mr Whittaker I know! I know! I know all about your little find. I wouldn't celebrate just yet. Our legal department won't have missed this. Wills can be overturned you know, particularly if all conditions haven't been adhered to.
Hilary What?
Mr Whittaker Well, apart from this nonsense tonight, when has there been any music or art here?
Mrs Weekly When I was girl, that's when.
Mrs Pagett There was music here all the time. Brass bands of a Wednesday, waltzes of a Sunday, Strauss waltzes, and hymns of a Sunday evening — in there.
Nick *(grinning)* Flora's Temple.
Mr Whittaker *(turning on Zoë)* I told you to keep an eye on him!
Zoë Yes Mr Whittaker.

Mr Whittaker Why the hell didn't you keep him away from here till it was all over!

Zoë I'm sorry Mr Whittaker, I tried, I really did.

Mr Whittaker (*to George*) You do realise what you've lost by fraternising with this lot I suppose?

George I'm just beginning to.

Nick You will still be coming to our play tomorrow, won't you? Champagne all round?

Mr Whittaker Oh yes, we'll be here all right — with the champagne.

Nick (*with a smile*) Good. Right! The sun's shining. It's a great day. What do we do now?

Charlotte I'll tell you what we do now. Our Dress Rehearsal! Everybody on stage for the opening number!

41: Finale. Summer in the Park (Music XXII)

Charlotte	Stand by the lights.
Nick	Stand by the actors.
The Company	Stand by the prompter.
	We're ready to go.
	Stand by on sound
	Stand by the techies
	This is the beginning of the show.

    This is the place
    This is the moment
    The weather's decent
    And it's getting dark.
    Focus your eyes
    Get ready to listen
    We'll tell you the story of Freshwater Park.

    The tale is true
    The people existed
    Flora and Harry
    William and Jack.
    This is the place
    Where it really happened.
    Make room for the latecomers up at the back.

    And if you think
    The story is touching
    And the place itself
    A bit of a lark,
    Lift up your voices
    And make a commotion.
    Don't let them bulldoze Flora's Walk.

    Nerves are on edge
    You can feel the tension

Sweat on our collars
But we're up to the mark.
So hit the lights
And bring on the action,
This is the opener of Summer in the Park,
Summer in the Park!

CURTAIN

FURNITURE AND PROPERTY LIST

ACT I

On stage:
Raised section
Stone steps encrusted with moss and debris
Rectangular hollow with a low stone-slabbed wall around it
Little empty ornamental pool. *In it*: rubbish
Broken statue
Graceful little eighteenth century "temple"
Low stone balustrade with broken urns
Two little curved decorative "shrines"
Little stone benches
Drinks cans, crisp packets, plastic bottles etc.
Damp mouldering mattress
Graffiti on stonework
Huge moon made from gauze or plastic

Off stage:
Bag of shopping. (**Mrs Weekly**)
Bag of shopping (**Mrs Pagett**)
Briefcase, polaroid camera (**Mr Whittaker**)
Fish-slice, dustbin bag (**Tom**)
Scraper, bag of newspapers (**jack**)
Scraper, dustbin bag (**William**)
Guitar (**Jack**)
Books, bags (**various members of the company**)
Bottle of lemonade (**Louise**)
Fan (**Emma**)
Skip. *In it*: jewelled masks, swords, boxing gloves, elegant brocade coat, whip, outrageous eighteenth century dresses, eighteenth century cream and gold dress wrapped in tissue paper
File, notebook, pen etc. (**Charlotte**)
File, notebook, pen etc. (**Nick**)
File, notebook, pen etc. (**Sophie**)
Refreshments (**Mrs Weekly**)
Rug (**Mrs Pagett**)
Portable tape recorder (**Liz**)
Bag. *In it*: piece of paper (*Liz*)
Camera (**Gary**)

Personal:
Mr Whittaker: business card
Old Lady: large brimmed straw hat, black silver topped stick

Furniture and Property List

ACT II

Strike: Rubbish, drinks cans, crisp packets, plastic bottles etc
Mattress
Graffiti
Costume skip

Set: String of coloured lights across the top of the temple lighting
Lighting notes, clipboard, script etc.
Material and equipment for a technical rehearsal
Large cardboard box. *In it*: handbills, programmes and publicity material

Off stage: Costume skip *In it*: plastic costume bags (**David and Michael**)
Pile of costumes (**David**)
Costume (**Emma**)
Cream and gold dress (**Sophie**)
Carpet bag (**Abigail**)
Reticule. *In it*: letter (**Flora**)
Bunches of flowers, including waterlillies (**Laura and Amy**)
Garlands of silver paper and crystal beads (**Jack, Tom and William**)
Costumes, lights, cables, props etc (**Chris and Michael**)
Little card table, several flasks of "red wine", "glasses",
Packs of cards, biscuits on a silver tray (**Louise and Emma**)
Props list (**Sue**)
Velvet screen (**Joanna and Sue**)
Four little chairs (**Joanna, Sue, Louise and Emma**)
Notebook (**Nicky**)
Plastic cup of coffee (**Katie**)
Sandwich (**Sophie**)
Newspaper (**David**)
Fairy lights, ladder (**Michael and Tom**)
Large bulging carrier bag. *In it*: letters, photographs, diaries, leather-bound book, small box. *In it*: jet necklace and a brooch, lace collar (**George**)

LIGHTING PLOT

ACT I
To open: Blue sky effect

Cue 1   **Katie** enters slowly   (Page 1)
Lights pale, glittering and mysterious

Cue 2   **Nick** and **Charlotte** enter   (Page 2)
Cross-fade to blue sky effect

Cue 3   **Sophie** and **Nick** exit in opposite directions   (Page 22)
Lights cross-fade to a misty grey dawn with the pink gold hint of a beautiful day.

Cue 4   **Tom, William** and **Jack** exit   (Page 25)
Lights slowly come up to a warm golden morning light

Cue 5   The **Old Lady** exits   (Page 25)
Lights come up full to a brilliantly sunny day

Cue 6   **Nick** moves DS to greet **Hilary**   (Page 34)
The lights fade slightly, except on the central tableau

Cue 7   **Katie** stands alone, watching the Old Lady   (Page 39)
Lights fade

ACT II
To open: Artifical stage light

Cue 8   **Charlotte**: "You can get out of those clothes now."   (Page 42)
Cut out moon and flood stage with brilliant light

Cue 9   **Tom** exits with the moon   (Page 42)
Cross-fade to a warm, gold, late afternoon light on the central area, while outside this area it is getting dark

Cue 10   **Katie, Sophie** and **Nick** stand still, a little sad   (Page 49)
Lights gradually get darker

Cue 11   **Katie, Sophie** and **Nick** seem unable to leave   (Page 49)
The moon begins to appear mistily from behind the temple

Cue 12   **Katie**: "Never leave, they whisper."   (Page 51)
Lights on the centre stage fade, leaving Sophie, Nick and Katie picked out by moonlight

Lighting Plot

Cue 13	**Nick** takes **Sophie's** hand and they exit *Black-out*	(Page 52)
Cue 14	There is a burst of noise and chattering *Bring lights up bright and sunny*	(Page 52)
Cue 15	**Charlotte:** "Positions please for the drinking scene." *Spotlight the card table*	(Page 54)
Cue 16	**David:** "Har Har Har." *Fade spotlight and bring up a pool of light by the fountain*	(Page 57)
Cue 17	**Danny, Mark** and **Michael** freeze *Lights up on Sophie*	(Page 57)
Cue 18	**Sophie:** "Abigail, is that you?" *Black-out*	(Page 57)
Cue 19	**Chris** stalks off *After a moment, a very prosaic work light comes up*	(Page 57)
Cue 20	**Chorus:** "We're getting angry!" *Lights come up suddenly to the state for Cue 15*	(Page 60)
Cue 21	**David, Michael, Mark** and **Danny** take their places *Repeat cue 16*	(Page 61)
Cue 22	The music fades away *Lights come up full*	(Page 66)
Cue 23	There is a very faint rumble of thunder in the distance *Lights fade slightly*	(Page 68)
Cue 24	The thunder and lightning die away *Lights continue to fade as the moon comes up*	(Page 71)
Cue 25	**Nick** slowly exits in the same direction Katie has taken *Lights come up full and blazing*	(Page 75)

EFFECTS PLOT

ACT I

Cue 1	**Sophie** and **Nick** exit in opposite directions *Dawn chorus*	(Page 22)

ACT II

Cue 2	**Nick:** "There is nothing to be sorry for!" *Cackle of geese*	(Page 48)
Cue 3	**Charlotte** turns away *Very faint rumble of thunder in the distance*	(Page 68)
Cue 4	**Tom** "Flora's walk." *Peal of thunder and the sound of heavy rain, which continues until Nick exits*	(Page 69)

www.ingramcontent.com/pod-product-compliance
Lightning Source LLC
LaVergne TN
LVHW051754080426
835511LV00018B/3313